VIENNA 1850–1930
ARCHITECTURE

VIENNA 1850–1930
ARCHITECTURE

Photography by Roberto Schezen
Text by Peter Haiko

RIZZOLI
NEW YORK

First published in the United States in 1992
by Rizzoli International Publications, Inc.
300 Park Avenue South, New York, NY 10010

Library of Congress Cataloging-in-Publication Data

Schezen, Roberto.
    Vienna 1850–1930, architecture / photographs by Roberto Schezen :
text by Peter Haiko : [translated from the German by Edward Vance
Humphrey].
        p.   cm.
    ISBN 0-8478-1324-X
    1. Architecture, Modern—19th century—Austria—Vienna—Pictorial
works.   2. Architecture, Modern—20th century—Austria—Vienna—
Pictorial works.   3. Architecture—Austria—Vienna—Pictorial
works.   4. Vienna (Austria)—Buildings, structures, etc.—Pictorial
works.   I. Haiko, Peter.   II. Title.
NA1010.V5S34   1992
720'.9436'1309034—dc20   92-3474
                                                                                        CIP

Translated from the German by Edward Vance Humphrey
Designed by Roberto Schezen with Mary McBride
Printed and bound in Hong Kong

Front and back covers: J. M. Olbrich, Secession Building, 1897–98
Frontispiece: Otto Wagner, Postsparkasse (Postal Savings Bank), 1904–07

Illustration Credits

*Numbers in roman refer to page numbers. Numbers in italics refer to illustration
numbers.*

Vienna Historical Museum: *1, 2, 5,* 7, *9, 13, 14, 15, 16, 23, 24, 29, 30,* 31,
37, 53, 57, 58, 61, 89, 101, 119, 123, 131, 165, 243

Institute for Applied Arts at the University of Vienna: *3, 4, 6, 8, 10, 11, 12,
17, 19,* 58, 59, 203

Federal Office of Monuments, Vienna: *32,* 253

CONTENTS

VIENNESE ARCHITECTURE 1850–1930   8

SYNAGOGUE, SEITENSTETTENGASSE   26

ARSENAL, WAFFENMUSEUM   30
Arsenal, Weapons Museum

PARLAMENT   36
Parliament

OPERA   52

MUSIKVEREIN   56
Musical Society

KUNSTHISTORISCHES MUSEUM   60
Art History Museum

BURGTHEATER   74

HAUS STURANY, SCHOTTENRING 21   78

PALMENHAUS   84
Palm House

GASOMETER   88
Municipal Gasworks

WASSERTURM   92
Municipal Water Tower

LÄNDERBANK   100

BRIDGE, WIENZEILE   106

HOFPAVILLON HIETZING   110
Court Pavilion at Hietzing

STATION KARLSPLATZ   118
Karlsplatz Station

BUILDINGS AT LINKE WIENZEILE 38 & 40   122

POSTSPARKASSE   130
Postal Savings Bank

KIRCHE AM STEINHOF   148
Steinhof Church

APARTMENT BUILDINGS AT NEUSTIFTGASSE 40—
DÖBLERGASSE 4   160

SECESSION BUILDING   164

PORTOIS & FIX BUILDING   174

ARTARIA BUILDING   178

ZACHERL BUILDING   182

HEILIGGEIST KIRCHE   192
Holy Spirit Church

ABSCHLUß DER WIENFLUßEINWÖLBUNG   198
Arch over the River Wien

SANATORIUM PURKERSDORF   202

VILLA SKYWA-PRIMAVESI   210

VILLA KNIPS   218

HAUS AM MICHAELERPLATZ   222
Building on the Michaelerplatz

HAUS SCHEU   232

CREMATORIUM   238

AMALIENBAD   242
The Amalien Baths

KARL MARX HOF   246

HAUS WENZGASSE   248

HAUS WITTGENSTEIN   252

ACKNOWLEDGMENTS

Professor Paolo Portoghesi, who, at the time of my studies at the Politecnico in Milan was the dean of the Faculty of Architecture, first encouraged me to look carefully into the cultural heritage of the Viennese Secession.

I want to thank Professor Hermann Czech in Vienna for his valuable advice and continuous care during the organization of this book.

Marlies Schrei has organized most of the shooting in Vienna; for this I thank her.

I am honored to have worked with Professor Peter Haiko; his understanding and knowledge of the Viennese architectural legacy have been key elements in this book, focusing on the links between neoclassical architecture and the Secession in Vienna.

I am grateful to David Morton at Rizzoli International for his editorial support and to Gianfranco Monacelli, president of Rizzoli International, for having encouraged this project.

VIENNESE ARCHITECTURE

1850–1930

"Der Zeit ihre Kunst—der Kunst ihre Freiheit" (To the Age, Its Art—To Art, Its Freedom). This motto over the entrance of the Vienna Secession Building, built by Joseph Maria Olbrich, describes the goals of Viennese modernism around 1900. The members of the Viennese artists' association called Secession, with Gustav Klimt as the president, resigned from the old, established Genossenschaft bildender Künstler Wiens (Viennese Cooperative of Fine Artists) in 1897, since their own progressive aims could not be reconciled with those of the established artists. Their primary accusation against adherents of the old school was that they were too rooted in the past and thus unable to create art appropriate to their own times. On a deeper level, this criticism meant a total rejection of—and an absolute break with—the art and culture of the second half of the nineteenth century, that is, the art and culture that still to a large extent characterize the architectural and cultural face of Vienna.

Thus, with respect to architecture, the demand "Der Zeit ihre Kunst" (To the Age, Its Art) was a condemnation of the architecture of the Viennese Ringstrasse, which suddenly stood accused of not satisfying contemporary needs, of not having developed any contemporary forms, and, as Otto Wagner and Adolf Loos put it, of having brought forth merely a Potemkin village, that is, something mendacious and false:

> Whenever I stroll along the Ring, it always seems to me as if a modern Potemkin had tried to perform the task of making someone believe he had been set down in a city full of aristocrats. Whatever Renaissance Italy produced in the way of lordly palaces was plundered in order...to conjure up a New Vienna that...might be inhabited by people in a position to own...an entire palace.[1]

The fault of the architecture of the Ringstrasse, they felt, was above all its enduring orientation toward the art of past epochs. For just this reason, the discussion of the Secession Building placed quite particular emphasis on the fact that "no detail" was patterned on "anything already in existence."[2] New art versus old became the subject of debate.

What artistic considerations characterize the architecture of the Ringstrasse? Why would these principles later come under such attack from the proponents of modernism?

"It is my will that the expansion of the inner city of Vienna should be taken up as soon as possible, and that consideration be given thereby to the regulation and beautification of my residence and the capital of my empire."[3] This famous command by Emperor Franz Joseph I marked the beginning of Vienna's transformation into a modern metropolis. The consequent razing of the medieval city walls created the space necessary for construction of the Ringstrasse, that magnificent boulevard which encircles the inner city with its numerous public buildings and shapes the face of Vienna to this day. Along with the medieval St. Stephen's Cathedral in the heart of the city, the Opera, the Burgtheater, and the Parliament building, among others, have become the architectonic synonym for Vienna.

Municipal expansions were carried out in most European cities, including Paris, Barcelona, Munich, and Cologne. The reasons for this were many. It was essential to make room for buildings that had become necessary for purposes of administration and ostentation, as well as for new housing; and, by razing the often medieval city fortifications, to permit unhindered contact between the old towns constricted within the walls and the ever more rapidly expanding outer precincts. The same applied in Vienna as well.

Militarily, the city walls had become obsolete with the advent of new weapons technology, as was demonstrated during Napoleon's siege of Vienna. However, there was another factor that came to outweigh such considerations, one conditioned above all by the civil revolution of 1848. There was now less fear of attack from outside than there was of the "inner" enemy; there was anxious talk of a "potential attack by the proletariat" from the outlying districts. There was a need, therefore, to guarantee the safety of the imperial court even after the fall of the old fortifications. The military authorities in Vienna deliberated for nearly ten years as to how this should be accomplished. Finally, they decided on the construction of a fortified triangle consisting of two barracks at either end of the Ringstrasse and the so-called Arsenal.

The latter, an enormous complex consisting of barracks, workshops, weapons depots, administration buildings, a rifle factory, and an artillery foundry, also encompassed a church and, first and foremost, the Waffenmuseum (weapons museum), conceived primarily as an Austrian hall of fame to glorify the deeds of the Austrian army and the most renowned commanders in Austrian history since the outbreak of the Thirty Years' War.[4] Built by Theophil Hansen, the weapons museum is, architecturally speaking, one of the earliest and most important buildings of Viennese historicism, characterized by its stylistic recourse to a number of prototypes. Still missing was a binding style that would serve as a model. In this regard, it was perhaps no accident that the models used in the Arsenal were combined very freely indeed. This raises the question, What might one have taken as a model for a building with such a specific function? A

1. The Ringstrasse, c. 1880

medieval fortification, perhaps? But that was precisely what was meant to be veiled, particularly in the weapons museum.

Conceived in 1857, the Ringstrasse was essentially completed in the 1870s and 1880s (fig.1). All the buildings, whether public or private, conform in their architectural appearance to historicist principles of design; that is, they refer back to older styles, especially in their formal details. Such references serve to imbue the architecture with a very specific expressive force. The architecture of Viennese historicism is a speaking architecture in that it always attempts to impart to the viewer something of the meaning and purpose of the building.

For the Parliament (fig. 2), regarded as an "august temple of the law," the architect Theophil Hansen chose the Greek style for this very reason. The architecture, praised as "magnificent and unique," was intended, in its "resplendent, graphic beauty, its nobly measured proportions, the harmonic

effect of its masses," as a national monument "which [would], as a splendidly ornamented abode of freedom," fill "future generations with high regard for its builders and embellishers."[5]

By thus invoking the past, a very specific statement was made for present and future. Each building was invested with the character of a monument. For example, the Vienna Rathaus (fig. 3), which was meant to express the "increasing prosperity of the bourgeoisie" and "in its outward appearance, in the development of its forms, and in its decorative furnishings is to be endowed with an appearance that exemplifies its extraordinary purpose."[6]

How one gives expression to the "increasing prosperity of the bourgeoisie" is demonstrated by the architecture of the Vienna Rathaus as it was actually realized. In general, the Gothic style was used as a model because the Gothic was seen as the epoch coinciding with "the first flourishing of the German

9

2. Theophil Hansen, Parliament, 1874–1883

5. Heinrich Ferstel, courtyard of the University of Vienna

4. Town Hall, Brussels

3. Friedrich Schmidt, Rathaus

6. Courtyard, Palazzo Farnese, Rome

bourgeoisie."[7] In the Rathaus, however, the confrontation with the stylistic model was not limited to mere formal details; rather, the significant form of the Rathaus's medieval precursor was appropriated by borrowing the central tower and arcades typical of this type of building. Of the Vienna Rathaus it has been written: "In order to give the Rathaus the typical character of this sort of building, the artist set in the middle of the façade a tower that develops independently from the base of the building."[8] The tower thus became a semiotic sign for "Rathaus." Moreover, since it is "of such height that it rivals that old emblem of the city of Vienna, the high tower of St. Stephen's,"[9] it was conceived as a new emblem for Vienna. The old religious monument had to compete with the new bourgeois building.

The intent of Friedrich Schmidt, the architect of the Vienna Rathaus, was not to make a superficial, stylistic copy but to create a building that would reveal

itself as the seat of the bourgeoisie's power and strength. To do this, he referred back to precisely those historical buildings from the epoch that "coincides with the flourishing of the German bourgeoisie." The recourse to a model, perhaps similar to the town hall of Brussels (fig. 4), and the quotation from a historic architecture legitimized contemporary claims to power; history thus served as proof of legitimacy. The claim to power, which was legitimized by means of the past, simultaneously manifested itself in the present and—in the form of architecture—was documented for all time to come.

In the University of Vienna (fig. 5), the architect Heinrich Ferstel quite consciously quoted the Renaissance in a fashion that made his contemporaries hear music; in their memories, "the great buildings of Italy [came] alive, and the lauded names of Bramante and San Michele and Sansovino, and all the rest from the golden age of the cinquecento" resounded in their ears.[10] Indeed, the arcade court of the university, the centerpiece of the whole complex, would be unthinkable without its artistic discourse with the court façades of the Palazzo Farnese, one of the greatest of the Renaissance palaces of Rome (fig. 6).

This was a very conscious and deliberate quotation from the Italian Renaissance, and the appropriation of form was an attempt to endow the architecture with a specific, telling content. The modern Renaissance was supposed to invoke and reawaken the Renaissance age as that time in which humanism first "took practical effect as a necessary element of everyday life,"[11] as Jacob Burckhardt phrased it. Given such considerations, it should be no surprise that the university, described as the "fount of knowledge," the seat and guardian of humanist thought, was built on the Ringstrasse in the style of the Renaissance (fig. 7).

Historicist architecture, more so than the architecture of any other epoch, is an architecture of intentional self-portrayal. This was not least because both the self-esteem of the individual and the self-image of the ruling classes had entered a crisis in the nineteenth century. Proof of this is found in the explicit urge to legitimize oneself—that ultimately impotent attempt to authenticate oneself, over and over again, by means of the past. Even, or perhaps especially, the imperial dynasty was not immune to this identity crisis. Even in the days of true sovereign power, that is, principally in the eighteenth century, the seat of the Hapsburgs, the Hofburg in Vienna, was de facto always under construction. New architectural components were constantly added to the already existing corpus. In the second half of the nineteenth century, a time when the Hapsburg monarchy was slowly but surely approaching its end, the Hapsburgs planned a total expansion of the imperial residence (figs. 8, 9), a gigantic forum complex, enlarging the residence to such an extent that a sensible use for the projected architecture was simply never found. In planning the expansion of the Hofburg during a time of growing bourgeois influence, the intent was to reestablish, in Vienna and for Vienna, and thus for the monarchy as a whole, the power of the imperial house by architectural means.

7. *Heinrich Ferstel, University of Vienna, 1873–84*

8. Semper and Hasenauer, ink drawing of the extension of the Hofburg

9. Semper and Hasenauer, photo of the extension of the Hofburg

The so-called Kaiserforum was supposed to stick out like a wedge into the democratic flow of the Ringstrasse, creating a very distinct caesura in the Ringstrasse. Triumphal arched gates were to have connected the planned segment wings of the so-called Neue Hofburg with the two museum buildings on the other side of the Ringstrasse; and the new Hofburg Theater was, in the original plan, to have been linked directly with the Hofburg complex. This would have been unmistakable testimony to the fact that public access to art collections and theater was entirely owing to the munificence of the Hapsburgs.

Like the Opera, Parliament, and Rathaus, among others, the Kunsthistorisches Museum was also a so-called monumental building—which was the highest-ranking architectural task in the whole of theoretical architectural thought in the latter half of the nineteenth century. Significantly enough, the terms *monumental building* and *public building* came to be equated:

Thus, government buildings, city halls, churches, schools, theaters, concert and music halls, and so on, are buildings of a public character, since the fact that everyone is entitled to frequent and use them gives them a public character. This kind of building is passed from one

generation to the next, and so, by attesting to the degree of education of the mind, to the standing, to the wealth, and to the greatness and power of the people who build them, they take on a commemorative and therefore monumental character, which is why they are more properly termed monumental buildings.[12]

The architectonic design with its richness of form, and the decorative design with its complicated iconological program—as, for example, in the Kunsthistorisches Museum—took on the task of monumentalization and exaltation. The architecture of the museum became the monument of a museum. The functional building became a cult building—an ecclesiastical building consecrated to art—whose purpose was to provide the works of art therein exhibited with a dignified framework and to put them beyond the realm of the everyday. The interior mise en scène made even the simple act of entering the building a dignified and solemn procession, elevating the visitor from the everyday level of the street into the realm of art. From the front steps one passed through a mighty set of portals and the imposing entrance foyer, and from there via a magnificent stairway to the all-dominating domed hall of the main floor. Only from there could one proceed to the individual collection halls. A very similar staging was found in the splendid stairways of the Opera and the Burgtheater.

But the Ringstrasse was not only the site of monumental public buildings, but also the domicile of Vienna's haute bourgeoisie; that is, of the new social stratum of bankers and merchants who had become immensely wealthy over a relatively short time (usually three generations), and to whom the newly created Ringstrasse offered the possibility of developing a style of life appropriate to their social status and representative of their position in society. The haute bourgeoisie, the so-called second Viennese society, generally only recently ennobled, constantly competed for status with the old nobility, the "first society." The latter always remained, for the former, an unattainable model. For instance, the portal of the house at Schottenring 21 (fig. 10) plainly recalls those of baroque palaces. By quoting a Viennese palace from the eighteenth century, the owner of Schottenring 21, an architect who grew rich with the building boom on the Ringstrasse, wished to set himself on a par with a baroque prince; the prince's claim to prestige, legitimized by history, was used to validate the intended claim to status of the nouveau riche builder. The house of the *arriviste* on the Ringstrasse made a claim to equality with a palace of the old nobility. Like a baroque noble's palace, therefore, the floor on which the owner himself lived was given particular emphasis, as the *bel étage* (second floor). The stories above and below it have less ornamentation on the façade, and smaller windows. This was supposed to indicate that the inhabitants of these levels were of lower social standing than the owner. The formal models for such a façade design were again provided by the old baroque palace. There, too, the particular emphasis was on the main floor, which usually contained the festival hall; there, too, the floors above and below, generally reserved for the servants, received less emphasis. But whereas one family resided in the aristocratic palace, the lord of the house (owner) of the elegant apartment building on the Vienna Ringstrasse lived on one floor only, while the others were rented out. The social differentiation in the aristocratic palace between masters and servants became a social differentiation between owner and tenants, made manifest by the architectonic-decorative structure of the façade. Inside the house there was often a luxurious stairway reserved exclusively for the owner and his visitors, while the tenants are expected to frequent a far less elegant staircase.

In the haut bourgeois apartment itself, owners strove for the grandeur necessitated by the competition for status, in order to procure the legitimacy demanded by their positions. The interior spatial layout of the apartment on the *bel étage* (fig. 11) showed, in turn, more or less plainly its dependence upon the aristocratic baroque city palace. At the center of the apartment, defining the claim made by the owner, was the ballroom; beside this, there was usually also a reception hall and a dining hall, at the least. Ballroom in the middle, flanked by even more ostensive rooms: this is precisely the canonical schema for the interior spatial arrangement in the public sphere of a palace. Only in the nineteenth century it had become significantly smaller, and thus an expression of the reduced publicness the bourgeoisie was able to develop in its ceremonial rooms. Unlike absolute rulers, they could not simply elevate each private event to an act of state.

While the Schottenring 21 building was oriented not only structurally but also stylistically to the forms of the baroque palace, the dominant style in Vienna during the 1870s and 1880s was generally neo-Renaissance. The development of the social stratum that ultimately set the trend in the era of the Ringstrasse (i.e., the period between 1860 and 1880–90), that is, the second society, quite logically and necessarily led to a renaissance of the Renaissance. This second society, made up of high officials, military officers, and above all bankers and wholesalers who had rapidly grown wealthy, pressed hard for social recognition, particularly for ennoblement. Although written with the social conditions of the Italian Renaissance in mind, the beginning of Jacob Burckhardt's chapter "Equalization of the Classes" reads like a report on conditions in Vienna at the time the first edition of his book *Die Kultur der Renaissance in italien: Ein Versuch* (The culture of the Renaissance in Italy: A study) appeared:

> Birth and origin still have influence only when combined with inherited wealth and secured leisure. This is not, in the absolute sense, to be understood such that the class categories seek to assert themselves now to a greater, now to a lesser degree....But the general trend of the period evidently ran toward a fusion of the classes in the sense of the newer world.[13]

In the Vienna of the Ringstrasse period, the newly ennobled haut bourgeois, the *Ritter von* (Knight of), born without the title that he generally earned by philanthropic activity, attempted to keep abreast of the old nobility. Burckhardt wrote:

> Upon closer examination, however, one realizes that this belated cult of knighthood independent of all hereditary nobility, while to some extent a matter of mere laughable, title-hungry vanity, does have another side to it. For the tournaments still continue, and he who would take part in them must, for form's sake, be a knight.[14]

There is at least this difference between the Renaissance as described by Burckhardt and the nineteenth century: the tournaments of the nineteenth century were no longer fought in the arena, but rather in the realm of commerce, at the bourse; in that of culture, at the museum and the university; and in that of

10. Bel étage *of Schottenring 21*

society, on the Ringstrasse, in the palace, and in the salon. Surrounded by the Renaissance, even if only in the form of copies and quotations, the citizen of the Ringstrasse elevated himself—of course only figuratively and in pretense—to the status of a Renaissance prince. In a restorative utopia he transported himself back to the time of the Italian Renaissance, equated—as wish-projection—his banking house in Vienna with that of the Medici in Italy, and so fulfilled his longing to be, like a Renaissance man, "the perfect social man" in the "outward refinement of life" and in the "higher form of sociability."[15]

Among the artists who confronted the Italian Renaissance, by no means the least significant is Otto Wagner. Both his monumental buildings from the 1880s and his apartments and villas are unthinkable without the discourse with the fifteenth and sixteenth centuries in Italy. The front of the Länderbank, which quotes a palazzo's façade (fig. 12), corresponds to the main hall inside (fig. 13),

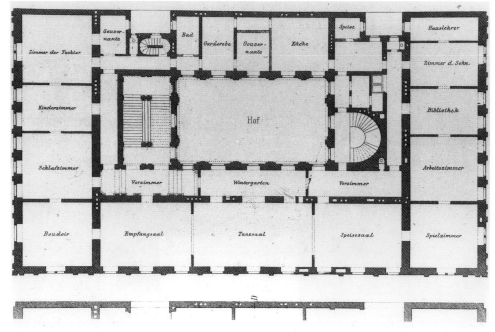

11. *Typical* bel étage *floor plan*

12. *Viennese baroque palace*

done in the style of Italian ecclesiastical architecture. With the aid of Renaissance forms, Wagner achieved an ennoblement and quasi-ecclesiastical exaltation of monetary transactions. The same thing, namely the orientation toward the art of the south, is demonstrated in individual residences, especially all in the so-called First Villa Wagner. This villa testifies to Wagner's artistic discourse with Andrea Palladio, whose villas were built for Venetian aristocrats of the sixteenth century. Like Palladio, Wagner realized in the First Villa an enclave outside the city, an enclave both in the ideality of the floor plan and in the overall conception—in the combination of architecture and landscape (fig. 14).

Ten years after building the First Villa, Wagner declared—at least theoretically—this Viennese style, this modern Renaissance, to be outgrown, and now only valid as the basis for new endeavors. In his book *Moderne Architektur* (Modern architecture), published in 1895, he wrote, "Yet so mighty is the

upheaval that we cannot speak of a renaissance of the Renaissance. A completely new birth, a *naissance* will proceed from this movement."[16] This new birth took the place of rebirth, incipient modernism replaced the Renaissance.

As early as 1890 Wagner made a radical break with historicism. He was by then convinced that one most definitely could not achieve a contemporary architecture by "seeing" the solution to the problem "in this or that style or [by making] certain stylistic movements serve specific architectural purposes."[17] In short, he condemned precisely that which—as has been demonstrated—was one of the the main principles of architecture in the latter half of the nineteenth century. According to his new credo, only the "evolution and transformation, along with the utilization of all motifs and materials," could lead to a new style.[18] Surveying his own artistic career up to that point, he noted, "The experiments with various styles hurried through by most of the architectural world in the last twenty years which, in more or less caricatured form, have consumed the building styles of millennia with the precipitousness of our way of life, have passed me by leaving little trace."[19] In his opinion, only "a certain liberal Renaissance that has absorbed our *genius loci* is, taking the greatest possible account of all our circumstances as well as of modern accomplishments in use of materials and construction, for present and future architecture the correct course."[20] He wrote this one year after the completion of the First Villa. Five years later, however, he rejected even this liberal Renaissance and finally arrived at a modern architecture.

The Majolikahaus at Linke Wienzeile 38 and 40 (fig. 15) of 1898–99 memorably demonstrates this shift in Wagner's architectural viewpoint. Outwardly, no one floor or apartment received special emphasis. The only reference to the historicist *bel étage* is the balcony on the third floor. The windows are all aligned along the same axes, floor after floor. The resulting serial structure corresponded with Wagner's theoretical reflection that "people's lifestyles, which daily grow more similar" had as their consequence the supplanting of the individual, single-family home by the "cell conglomerate." Surely it was not the serial rows that primarily impress the viewer, but quite the reverse: the unmistakable (and materially costly) artistic individuality of the houses Linke Wienzeile 38 and 40.

Each floor, each apartment participated equally in the prestige-value of the overall façade. No one apartment was outwardly individualized and set apart from the others as a special apartment for a special resident; rather, every apartment was presented to the street as equal in the aggregate, yet at the same time equally exclusive. The individual, de-individualized in the façade, disappeared behind the façade's masking exclusivity. To this extent, Wagner's conception made the increasing anonymity of the bourgeois individual around 1900 more than manifest: he withdrew behind the façade, into the interior. (For this reason, the interior was never so important as in the period around 1900.) Such masking of the individual was declared to be positively desirable by Adolf Loos: "The intelligent modern person must have a mask for people. Only the intellectually limited have the need to cry out to all the world what they are and how they actually are."

All the apartments became equal in standing, according to Wagner, not least because of the installation of an elevator: it was precisely this feature that guaranteed each apartment almost identical living quality. "Since, moreover, the rental value of the individual floors has been nearly equalized by the addition of passenger elevators, the natural consequence had to be that the differentiation of

13. Otto Wagner, Länderbank main hall, 1882–84

construction.

The artistic intention to make the structural visible and to make technological production plain became one of Wagner's main preoccupations after 1900. The architect faced the Postsparkasse (Postal Savings Bank) and Kirche am Steinhof (Steinhof Church) buildings with thin marble slabs. In doing so, he took up an idea already noted in his book *Moderne Architektur,* namely that the modern style of building sets itself apart from that of the Renaissance in that it does not pile one layer of stone atop another "with a large expenditure of time and money," but rather "uses slabs...as the outer facing for the building." The result of this method was, for Wagner, satisfactory in several respects: "The monumental effect is heightened by the superior material, the pecuniary means thus expended are enormously reduced, and construction time is held down to a usual, normal, and desirable level."[22]

But these considerations alone did not determine the façades of the Postal Savings Bank (fig. 17) and the Steinhof Church (fig. 18). The essential thing was that the modern style of cladding was presented unmistakably to the viewer— presented by means of the aluminum ornamental bolts that anchored the slabs. Their apparent function was to mark the structurally important points, however, the slabs were firmly embedded in mortar, thus requiring no additional anchoring. The bolts, as already noted by contemporary observers, were "a most modern and original ornament," purportedly dictated "by necessity."[23]

The aim was not to make visible the structure as such, but to make visible that which recalled it. The economical, time-saving aspects of the chosen structure were meant to remain manifest for all time to come. Thus each of the fifteen thousand bolts on the façade of the Postal Savings Bank has been invested with memorial character; not its real function is declared, but its ideal. And so, too, the bolts are distributed over the façade decoratively, according to purely artistic considerations. They are concentrated in the optically and architecturally significant central projection, thus emphasizing and ennobling this part of the building over those that flank it.

This new decor was intentionally quite different from the decorative forms of earlier epochs. Whereas, until then, the task of ornament had been to exalt the utilitarian form as art form, this decoration purported to be exclusively the result of structure. Rather than the decorative ornamentation of structure, there was structurally motivated decoration. From that time on, Wagner's architectural intent was to confront the viewer optically with a utilitarian form by means of the art form. Significantly, in so doing he did not necessarily make transparent the real conditions of creation, such as the actual construction; often he put in their place the aesthetic appearance. Thus, for Wagner, the simulation of an anchoring of the façade slabs was more important than their actual fastening. Perception took priority. This viewpoint alone permitted Wagner to make structure and function visible as symbolic form. His functionalism was a metaphorical one.

Almost compulsively, he put the management of technical-functional problems in the foreground. Often he wasted not a word about his architectural-artistic design, but devoted whole passages to the economic and technical advantages of individual considerations. For instance, he proffered the slabs of opaque white glass inside the Postal Savings Bank (fig. 19), also held in place by aluminum bolts, for the durable protection they gave the walls, since, after all, it was "a matter of experience that bank employees and customers are very prone to using the walls of such buildings for making financial calculations."[24]

the floors by outward artistic design was no longer advisable."[21] Therefore, the architect bestowed special attention upon the artistic design of the elevator. The elevator took on the task formerly assigned to the lavish stairways of the Ringstrasse residences which led exclusively to the *bel étage* of the owner. With the elevator, each apartment (as an equally entitled *bel étage* apartment) received its aesthetically exquisite, technologically state-of-the-art, therefore mechanized, splendid stairway. In place of the noble stairway for one individual was the elevator, which ennobled one and all. The division between the ennobled building owner and the other tenants did not, as in the Ringstrasse palace, begin in the vestibule. In the contemporary apartment building, all were equally noble.

The Viennese apartment building of the early modernist period would be unthinkable without Wagner's deliberations on matters of principle, which he modified yet again in 1910 to meet contemporary demands in his last two apartment houses, Neustiftgasse 40 (fig. 16) and Döblergasse 4. Both the so-called Zacherlhaus by Josef Plecnik, a student of Otto Wagner, and the Portois & Fix Building by Max Fabiani, an employee at Wagner's studio, can only be explained by referring back to Wagner's concept of modern apartment-building

14. Otto Wagner, First Villa Wagner

Wagner attempted to cancel the distinction made in the nineteenth century between civil engineers and architects. In those days, all essential new architectural tasks increasingly fell to the technical engineer; even in more traditional fields he played an ever more dominant role. The architect, by contrast, was appreciably losing ground. At best he was permitted to design the architectonic details of the new technical solutions. In his work for the Vienna Stadtbahn, Otto Wagner himself was originally given merely the task of putting "the stone masses and iron structures...into forms pleasing to the eye and not affronting to the aesthetic sense."[25] His successful endeavors to see that "no railway station, no depot, no viaduct arch, no bridge...be contracted out that [is] not designed artistically and modernly in the studio"[26] was merely a reflex, no matter how he strived and succeeded in reconquering territory previously lost to the architect. His intention was to unite in his architecture the realism of the engineer and the idealism of the architect. For him, structure was the "primordial cell of architecture . . . for without it no art form can arise." The "task of art" was

"to idealize that which exists."[27] Only the architect, however, could grasp the primal thought behind each structure, for each structure is ultimately something invented, that is, creative, and thus, at root, artistic.

Otto Wagner's prime demonstration of how modern technology and contemporary architecture could combine to form the ideal "architecture of our age" was the main hall of the Postal Savings Bank. In itself, the tripartite, basilican system of this room—a higher central nave accompanied by lower side aisles—characterized the ecclesiastical building in historical architecture. In the nineteenth century, however, it was also used in designs for railway stations, market and exhibition halls, and factories. Something always noticeable in the latter is that, despite ornamentation added after the fact, the form was often an inevitable result of the structure: for example, the continued visibility of crossbeams and tie rods. The developing aesthetic form remained readable as a consequence of the technically necessary structure.

Wagner, by contrast, made the actual structure only partially visible. He

15. Otto Wagner, Majolikahaus, 1898–99

16. Otto Wagner, Neustiftgasse 40, 1909–11

17. Otto Wagner, Postal Savings Bank facade, 1904–07

18. Otto Wagner, Steinhof Church, 1904–07

20. Postal Savings Bank glass ceiling

21. Interior of Steinhof Church

22. Otto Wagner, Doblergasse 4, 1911–12

19. Otto Wagner, Postal Savings Bank interior, 1904–07

and his de-materialization of the upper spatial boundary. Technical possibilities permitted him free quotation from a historical solution.

As a modern architect, Wagner attempted to provide his creation with a rational basis in order to give foundation to the art form as the necessary and sole result of the practical form. With the quotation from ecclesiastical architecture, he elevated the banking business above the level of the profane. This end was also served by the way in which the rooms leading to the main hall were staged: open-air stairway—portal—lobby—cross corridor—hall, with the tellers' windows, as it were, as side chapels; this arrangement emphasized the sanctity of the main room, ennobling it. With the quotation from a machine shop (also immanent in the spatial solution) he perfected the banking business, perfected it in the way work in the machine shop was tailorized.

In regard to his Steinhof Church (fig. 21), it is surprising that Otto Wagner emphasized the practical and useful elements of his plan, given that the church was the architectural crown of the Sanatorium and Home for the Mentally and Neurologically Ill. He noted that the floor, because it sloped gently toward the altar, was especially easy to clean. The new design of the holy-water fonts helped prevent infections. The short pews let attendants intervene at any time, and the triple portals permitted separate entry for male and female patients. That the layout of the church allowed "all visitors to see the high altar, and to see and especially to hear the priest" almost goes without saying.

Above all, Wagner presented his concept for the Steinhof Church as an ideally thought-out fulfillment of function, believing that this would gratify the

permitted the supports of the glass ceiling their optical effect, indeed gave them added emphasis by means of a technoid design (fig. 20). However, Wagner caused the glass ceiling itself to hover weightlessly and, as it were, immaterially above the room. The actual structural framework was indiscernible, remaining hidden behind or rather above the shell of the room, the upper limit of which was defined as a continuously shining, seemingly luminescent ceiling. The structure that actually supports the ceiling is located above this glass skin. The room's fascination lies partly in its sham presentation of the structural without making the structure visible. In the main hall of the Postal Savings Bank, Wagner quoted an ecclesiastical architecture with his adoption of the basilican schema

23. Cover of architecture magazine

order to make this circumspection comprehensible, Wagner gave the fastenings of the sheet metal an optically and haptically overarticulated effect, causing the portal to take on an overall apotropaic character. It shows the interior to be protected in an almost armorlike fashion. Only those worthy of the key, it seems to say, shall be permitted to enter this house.

The utterly smooth façades of the two buildings at Neustiftgasse 40 and Döblergasse 4 promulgate once again the up-to-date. Without any sort of conventional architectural ornament, with windows merely cut into the wall, these façades seem to have been designed just like those of the Loos house on the Michaelerplatz. Nevertheless, there are several principles of design that distinguish Wagner's solution from that of Adolf Loos. By means of horizontal and vertical grooves in the plasterwork, Wagner achieved the optical impression of a façade clad in slabs. This grid effect reinforces the impression of the serial, left-to-right and top-to-bottom ordering of uniform cell conglomerates, emphasizing the arbitrariness in this additive joining together.

Undoubtedly in reaction to the vehement discussion of the role of ornament and to the demand for renunciation of decor, Wagner realized his idea of an ornamentless façade and, remaining true to his stance of symbolic functionalism, combined it with the optical-symbolic suggestion of slab cladding. De facto, however, he returned in 1910—just as did Loos—to an honest mortar coating.

The period around 1900, already celebrated by contemporaries as a new departure, as modernism, was at the same time the period of crisis in ornament. The meaning and purpose of ornament were not only up for discussion, but also, by individuals such as Adolf Loos, flatly negated. The litmus test of "modernism" was, How do you stand on ornament? Modernism's critique of decor implied a general settling of accounts with the historicism of the latter half of the nineteenth century. Blows struck against ornament were aimed at the style. Thus the reversion to past forms that took place in historicism—primarily, of course, as an appropriation of historical decorative form—was blamed on ornament's unacceptable availability for the purpose. The style's inherent reproduction of the past was criticized in terms of the potential repetition of ornament. And, regardless of whether it was produced by industrial means or crafted by hand, historicist ornament is rated as machine-made ornament:

Precisely because the machine has lent itself to making ornaments on a mass scale, the entire art industry has experienced a flood of second-rate ornament, which has lowered artistic standards to a lamentable level. The ornament dumped on the market by the millions was bound to result in a devaluation. Ornament became vulgar. And, as a result of the developments in industrial arts over the past few decades, the person of taste has accumulated such an aversion to this mechanically produced ornament that it can no longer be borne.[28]

Ornament became the enemy:

If the thoughtful contemporary, deeply galled, even saddened, by today's riotous culture of the visible, asks himself seriously what is the reason that the world, insofar as it is the work of man, has become so very ugly and embarrassing, the answer to be had, provided he possesses sharp eyes and some facility for enjoying the beautiful, is: The enemy is ornament.[29]

standards of the general public. His specific artistic standard was made clear on the cover of a Viennese architectural journal designed by one of his students (fig. 23). It shows, superimposed, a classical temple, St. Peter's in Rome, and the Steinhof Church. This is meant to illustrate, in a kind of "genealogical tree of Jesse," the genesis of the Steinhof Church as aesthetic-artistic creation of form. Wagner achieved his solution in confrontation with classical architecture and with that of Michelangelo: the portal is to be read as a new interpretation of the temple façade, the dome form understood as a free quotation from St. Peter's. Based on the architecture of classical antiquity, with the authority of Michelangelo, Wagner's church rises up as the crown, the perfection—the incarnation of the "architecture of our age."

To an ever greater degree, Wagner's architecture took on the character of an *architecture parlante,* one meant to suggest to every viewer the artist's response to external necessities. For example, the oversized and overly numerous rivets on the portal to his last apartment building, Döblergasse 4 (fig. 22), were meant to hit home to both the viewer and the user: upon mature consideration, this entrance door has been protected against heedless damage with aluminum sheeting. In

25. Adolf Loos, building on the Michaelerplatz, 1910–12

HOHEWARTE

Biedermeier-Salon. Aquarell aus der Zeit um 1820.

Aus dem Besitze des Herrn Dr. Aug. Heymann.

145

24. *Biedermeier als Erzieher article, 1900*

For this reason Adolf Loos postulated: "The modern man, the man with modern nerves, does not need ornament, quite the reverse, he detests it. All objects that we call modern have no ornament."[30]

Thus, with the transformation, in the latter half of the nineteenth century, from craftsmanship to industrial art, ornament became vulgar, that is to say, common—in more than one sense of the word. The mass production of decorations for the masses spelled the end of the exclusiveness of the individual product for the individual. Ornament lost its original, ennobling function. Historically, decorative form was assigned the task of manifesting (artistic) value that went beyond pure utilitarian functionality. Preindustrial ornament lent the object an aura of sensuality. It individualized an object by virtue of its own individuality, thus ensuring an aura of the unique.

Adolf Loos was fully aware of the original function of ornament as a manifestation of status and social class, and he proceeded to transfer this role to the material itself: "One must bear in mind that precious materials and good workmanship do not merely compensate for lack of ornament; rather, they are far superior in their capacity to delight."[31] For him, the new art form came into being not by applying decoration to the functional form, but by utilizing a specific form and exquisite materials worked with first-class craftsmanship. The material alone, the naturally beautiful, was to become the new, artistically

beautiful object. Well-crafted, high-quality material excluded ornament, "for today, even the most degenerate person will think twice before decorating a fine wooden surface with marquetry." The very appreciation of the value of the material resulted in the renunciation of ornament. Loos believed that such renunciation would liberate capital wasted on ornament for worthwhile investment in valuable materials. "Ornament is squandered work, and therefore squandered health. So it always was. Today, however, it also means squandered material: and both mean squandered capital."[32]

The tendency to dispense with ornament altogether, or to reduce traditional ornament, led Loos as well as other proponents of Viennese modernism back to the period around 1800, a time when "abstinence from ornamental embellishment [had become] the source of new ideas [and when] the slavish dependence on a set of forms that maintained a merely artificial life" was left behind.[33] Incipient modernism saw its ideals already realized at the turn of the nineteenth century. The Biedermeier period became its model, its preceptor. "Biedermeier als Erzieher" (Biedermeier as educator)—such was the title of several articles appearing in progressive art journals circa 1900 (fig. 24). The desired abstention from ornament, raised to the level of high quality and exalted as an aesthetic of renunciation, was now seen as having been exemplarily anticipated in the period around 1800. Here, for the modernists, lay the lost paradise of artistic craftsmanship before the fall caused by the advent of industrial arts. Around 1800, said Loos, there was no longer the "sadism of the eighteenth century that saddled its fellow men with superfluous work. . . .[O]rnament means extra work."[34] But also around 1800 there was as yet no mass production that only made a pretense of being handcrafted. For Loos, therefore, planning his building on the Michaelerplatz (fig. 25), one thing was sure: "Now that I was finally vouchsafed the task of building a house...I had to pick up where the chain of developments had been broken"—namely the period around 1800.[35]

As early as 1898, Loos was referred to as a "killer of ornament,"[36] a new Saint George, so to speak, out to liberate the virgin (that is, architecture) from the evil dragon of ornament. He saw himself as a fearless warrior who, by means of his untiring battle against ornament, finally opened the way for mankind's cultural development. With missionary zeal he proclaimed: "The path of culture leads from ornament to ornamentlessness."[37] In his article "Ornament und Verbrechen" (Ornament and crime) he declared ornament to be the expression of an unbridled instinctual life. For him it was clear: "All art is erotic. The first ornament ever created, the cross, was erotic in origin. A horizontal line: the reclining woman. A vertical line: the man penetrating her."[38] Again and again, Loos addresses the sensuality, the libido inherent in and proceeding from ornament. Sensuality and libido were treated as an uncontrollable and therefore dangerous threat.

Viewed superficially, Adolf Loos's theory is similar to those of Sigmund Freud. In "Ornament und Verbrechen" Loos wrote, "The evolution of culture is synonymous with the removal of ornament from everyday objects."[39] Almost at the same time, Freud wrote, "Our culture is quite generally built upon the suppression of instincts. Renunciation has been progressive in the course of cultural development." And further: "Those whose unbending constitution will not allow them to go along with this suppression of instinct stand (opposed) to society as 'criminals,' as 'outlaws.' "[40] Compare this with Loos's verdict: "But those in our times who, prompted by an inner urge, smear the walls with erotic symbols [ornaments] are criminals or degenerates."[41] The fundamental difference between the two positions lies in this: for Freud, instinct remained (despite the necessity for control) the essential driving force in the development of the ego, whereas Loos saw suppression or even absolute renunciation of instinct (which, translated into the language of architecture, meant lack of ornament) as the one and only path to real humanity.

Again and again, Loos made the connection between ornament and femininity: "All objects that we call modern are unornamented...with the exception of the things that belong to woman."[42] Or: "Wherever we abuse everyday objects ornamentally, we shorten their life-spans. This murder of material can only be justified by the caprice and ambition of woman—for ornament in the service of woman will live forever....But the ornament of woman corresponds in essence to that of savages; it has erotic significance."[43] Fear of the eroticism of the mature woman became the rejection of ornament, of that ornament which, according to Loos, lived forever in the service of woman, murdered material, had erotic significance and, ultimately, belonged to the stage of barbarism, to the savages, to "the Papuans."

For Loos, lack of ornament became a symbol of intellectual power and, moreover, of the victory of Eros over "unnatural" sensuality. Lack of ornament was sublimated sensuality, to be enjoyed as a kind of ascetic beauty by those who lived "at our level of culture." Only to those who had not yet attained the height of culture, who still could not go to hear "Beethoven or Tristan after the toil and trouble of the day"[44] did Loos concede the right to ornament; that is, besides women, to Kaffirs, Persians, Slovakian peasant women and his shoemaker, "for all of them have no other means with which to scale the heights of their existence." On the other hand, dissociating himself from "those who require ornament," he proclaimed, "[We] have the art that has gone beyond ornament."[45]

The building on the Michaelerplatz, his "first house" as Loos himself proudly called it, became the manifestation of all his theories. This is an architecture stripped of any and all traditional ornament. Loos designed the façade to be entirely smooth and ornamentless. The two-storied business zone underneath was clad in marble; in the living area above he used the "honest plasterwork," applied by hand, which was the only thing he would even consider. With this conception he clearly distinguished the two different spheres, private and business, of the building: namely, the public, visible sphere of sales below, which clearly set itself apart from the anonymous sphere of private life above. Here, again clearly dissociating himself from historicist conventions—Loos put into architectural practice the notion, already quoted above, that the intelligent person would withdraw behind the façade into the interior, having no need at all to announce his name and station to outsiders. The façade became a speechless, veiling mask. This is why contemporary critics repeatedly labeled the Michaelerplatz building, among other things, the "house without eyebrows"—and thus without the essential characteristics of a face.

With this architectural demonstration of his reflections, Loos reaped furious protests. Construction had to be halted, and there was even talk of providing the façade, after the fact, with ornamentation. All too provocative was the effect, repeatedly objected to, of the façade's "nudity." Over and over, the façade of the Loos building was associated with the naked body of a woman; it was also described as smooth, indeed smooth-shaven. However, "Even enthusiastic nudists know how to distinguish between an uncouth, bosomy harlot and an ideally beautiful woman."[46] In view of the traditional garb of the surrounding stately and ecclesiastical architecture, so much nakedness, nakedness of a specific kind—in itself already "indecent, arousing, and horrifying"—was bound to be seen as particularly misplaced. Moreover, the architect was accused of intentionally misleading the public: "In his blueprints he pretended that he was going to 'decorate,' but when carrying them out he was caught by the building authorities in flagrante delicto, building uncannily smooth marble walls."[47] The publication of what was supposed to be private was seen as a public nuisance. In this regard, Loos himself remarked: "[My house] caused a real nuisance and the police promptly appeared at the scene. Such things might be perpetrated behind closed doors, they said, but they do not belong on the street!"[48]—especially not on ground held to be so "sanctified by art, tradition, and history."[49]

Josef Hoffmann and the Wiener Werkstätte were always an essential target for Loos's critical attacks. Whereas Loos, aided by the so-called spatial plan (Raumplan) which he developed, attempted first of all to meet the individual, private needs of those who would live in his villas, giving each room the appropriate dimensions, for Josef Hoffmann the problem of the Gesamtkunstwerk (total work of art) and its outward, public character always stood in the center of his reflections. Around 1900 the idea of the Gesamtkunstwerk—itself an intention going back at least as far as the baroque—became, primarily owing to Josef Hoffmann and the Wiener Werkstätte, the Übergesamtkunstwerk. It was no longer enough simply to make a building of a piece inside and out, that is, borne of a single artistic will, uniquely and unmistakably conceived; rather, the designer's will included and encompassed what was previously disregarded. Not only was the furniture itself to be stringently adapted to correspond with the style of the interior decoration, but also vases, slipcovers, tablecloths, and dinner utensils; indeed, even the clothing of the lady of the house was expected to subordinate itself to this all-penetrating stylistic principle. Be it the interior of a villa or the furnishings for a sanatorium, Hoffmann impressed upon each and every object his personal artistic style, thus ensuring his hegemony as the creator of a Gesamtkunstwerk. This compulsiveness seemed to preclude the actual usefulness of some of these interiors; one thinks, for instance, of the furnishings for Hoffmann's Palais Stoclet in Brussels. It must be asked whether this rigid

26. Josef Hoffmann, Villa Knips, 1924–25

27. Adolf Loos, Haus Scheu, 1912–13

aesthetization of everyday life still permitted life to be everyday. Adolf Loos, for one, made plain his opposition to this type of *Übergesamtkunstwerk*. In his tale "of a poor, rich man," he had nothing but scorn and derision for the intentions of the architect who believed it necessary to determine each and every object in the living quarters of the rich man. The result, for Loos, was that ultimately the poor inhabitant was left with no room for living.[50] Against this tendency Loos once again posited the example of the period around 1800. In his opinion, it was not the style of the architect that determined the style of the apartment, but the style of those who lived there. "Each piece of furniture, each thing, each object told a story, the story of the family. The apartment was never finished. To be sure, there was no style in it, that is, no foreign style. But the apartment had a style, the style of its inhabitants, the style of the family."[51]

Stylistically speaking, Josef Hoffmann—after a brief Jugendstil period, with its sweeping forms and floral ornamentation—evolved around 1904 a geometrical form-language which explained why he was given the sobriquet Quadrate-Hoffmann. Finally, around 1910, this tendency toward the additive chessboard pattern was combined with an ever more strongly expressed classicism, such as can be seen, for instance, in the façades of the Villa Skywa-Primavesi (fig. 28). This development corresponds with a general trend in European architecture in the last few years before World War I; one has only to think of the buildings of such men as J. M. Olbrich or Peter Behrens.

If one compares the architecture of the Villa Scheu by Adolf Loos (fig. 27) with that of the Villa Skywa-Primavesi, or, even better, of the Villa Knips (fig. 26), both by Josef Hoffmann, then something else—apart from the differing principles heretofore discussed—becomes conspicuous. Whereas Loos professed to build exclusively from the inside out, making the façade appear to be solely the result of the interior structure, Hoffmann more or less designed each front for itself. His frontages do not define themselves as the outward boundaries of a three-dimensional architectural cubature, but each one, by itself, as a picture painstakingly composed and framed.

After World War I, the construction of private residential buildings came

28. Josef Hoffmann, Villa Skywa-Primavesi, 1913–15

almost to a standstill as a result of the political-financial situation in general and in particular the specific taxation policy of the then Social Democratic city government. The Social Democrats declared the creation of housing space to be one of their foremost political aims. This was meant to eliminate private housing speculation and above all to provide decent living quarters for the workers as well. Generally speaking, the Social Democratic standpoint was that "residential housing (was) a public obligation, just as, earlier, the erection of school buildings and hospitals was a task for municipal or state welfare."[52] But the object was not to build just any apartments, "but to execute them in a form and manner corresponding to the spirit of the times and modern hygienic and artistic standards."[53] In 1923 the municipal administration passed a resolution calling for the creation of twenty-five thousand apartments within five years. Another program calling for thirty thousand apartments was adopted in 1927. By 1933 the Municipality of Vienna had erected roughly sixty thousand apartments and was thus in possession of around ten percent of all the apartments in Vienna.

Most plans involved so-called superblocks, such as the Karl Marx Hof (fig. 29) with its nearly fourteen hundred apartments. It should be emphasized that in matters of architectural design the builders did not follow the trends of modernism, of the *Neues Bauen* (New architecture), but rather remained bound to tradition. New technologies, too, were hardly utilized. This is understandable considering that the housing construction program was simultaneously intended to create jobs; new, rational, work-saving methods of construction were purposely excluded. In external appearance, the residential buildings of the Municipality of Vienna were intended to compete with the buildings of the nineteenth-century bourgeoisie:

> The Municipality of Vienna has entered a vigorous new phase of construction, one that compares in scope with the building of the Ringstrasse. Then, the State adorned its capital with palaces, museums, and architectural monuments; today, the City of Vienna is its own builder, and its creations are guided by social considerations alone.[54]

The concept behind many municipal buildings confirmed this intentional confrontation with and appropriation of the formerly feudal, grand-seigneurial architecture, along with its pathos formulae, which was employed by the bourgeoisie in the nineteenth century. For instance, quotations from the baroque—especially in terms of the urban architecture of the large complexes—were made to validate the Social Democrats' claim to power, while at the same time giving expression to their newly won self-image. The strong tendency to axial alignment, which so often, as in the Karl Marx Hof, found its monumentalized midpoint in a central court, sought to project an impression of power. This can be seen in particularly exaggerated form in the Karl Seitz Hof (fig. 30), for instance. The main courtyard is transformed into a gigantic exedra arrangement; the building complex itself is in a strictly axial relationship to the inner main street; and the middle section is elevated, with a tower and an imposing round-arched portal and accompanying pedestrian passageways. This structure, taken from castle architecture, corresponds to multistory ceremonial halls with balconies situated above the portal.

Josef Frank exposed the quotation character of this architecture, and the ideology behind it, as early as 1926. "Behind this we suddenly see again a whole principle reappearing, that of the unprincipled petite bourgeoisie. A principle which, using the palace for its stronghold, has preserved intact into our times its drive for prestige, at the cost of housing culture." And, as if making excuses, he continued: "Certainly, we could not go any other way. Our model happened to be the aristocratic palace, Vienna's only valuable architectural monument; but along with it went a culture that is not our own, one that comes from above, not from below, and that has no basis anymore."[55]

The architectonic design of almost all the buildings commissioned by the Municipality of Vienna was based on the following principles: expressivity of the

29. Karl Ehn, Karl Marx Hof, 1927–30

30. Hubert Gessner, Karl Seitz Hof

emphatically massive main body, monumental portal architecture on the one hand, spacious and extensive inner gardens on the other. This combination achieved a dual effect: it brusquely repelled the outsider by the diminishing effect of its architectural *force majeure*, while suggesting to the inhabitants protection and security against a "hostile" environment the moment they crossed the mighty round-arched portal. Upon stepping into the courtyard they entered a new environment, their own. Thus these buildings largely parallel the political position of Vienna's Social Democrats at that time. They were powerful, but were

31. Josef Frank, Haus Wenzgasse, 1930

32. Ludwig Wittengenstein and Paul Engelmann, Haus Wittengenstein, 1926–28

not (or could not be) certain of that power, as history later substantiated. It is significant that architecture was enlisted to help articulate and realize the wish and need for protection against the outside. Inhabitants were meant to be able to withdraw into a building in order to create their own self-contained, autarchic enclave. This conception corresponded exactly to that of the social-utopian architectural plans of the early nineteenth century; there were references in a formal sense as well. Suffice it to mention the parallels between Charles Fourier's Phalanstère and the Karl Marx Hof by Karl Ehn, who, like many other architects of Vienna's social housing projects, was a former pupil of Otto Wagner.

Whereas in the residential buildings the tendency toward expressive design often conflicted with the need to create as much housing space as possible, in Klemens Holzmeister's crematorium, also commissioned by the Municipality of Vienna, the architect succeeded in creating a building whose theatricality and pathos made it unique in Austria, the magnum opus of expressionist architecture of the 1920s. With the perfection of the Gothic, which manifests itself in expressionism generally, Holzmeister managed to create a solemn architecture with a freshly formulated sanctity and monumentality.

Besides Adolf Loos, one of the most important proponents of modernism was Josef Frank, who represented a quite independent and original variation on the architecture of the 1920s. His modernism, however, served as a counterpoint to modernism proper. In Haus Wenzgasse (fig. 31), Frank realized his thoughts on the "house as path and place":

A well-organized house should be laid out like a city, with streets and paths which inevitably lead to places that are cut off from the traffic, so that one can take a rest in them....A well-laid-out house resembles those fine old cities wherein even the stranger immediately knows his way around, and, without having to ask his way, finds the town hall and the marketplace.

Frank found methodically and rationally planned apartments without life, lacking "large rooms, large windows, numerous nooks, crooked walls, steps and differing levels, columns, and rafters." In his opinion, the modern residential building had much in common with the bohemian studio under the mansard roof. The task of the architect, he thought, was to order all these elements of the attic studio into a house.[56] Given such a basic attitude, it is not surprising that Frank later set his accidentism against the "conformist tendencies in modernism" and the "parade of forms in the new functionalism." He claimed that "we should design our surroundings as though they were created by chance....What we need is variety, not stereotypical monumentality. No one feels at home in an order that is forced upon him....Away with universal styles, away with the whole complex of ideas that has become popular under the name of functionalism."[57]

"To build a house would also greatly interest me," wrote the philosopher Ludwig Wittgenstein in a letter to Paul Engelmann, a former student of Adolf Loos. Engelmann was commissioned by Ludwig's sister, Margarethe Stonborough-Wittgenstein, to plan the Haus Wittgenstein (fig. 32) in 1926. Though an architectural autodidact, the philosopher was called in as a consulting architect by his sister in the autumn of 1926, and he signed the definitive plans "Ludwig Wittgenstein, Architect." This was preceded by the architectural-artistic dethroning of Engelmann by Wittgenstein. "Engelmann had to give way to the much stronger personality, and the house was then built, down to the smallest detail, according to Ludwig's plans and under his supervision." We are told with what meticulousness the philosopher planned each detail, and what precision he demanded in their execution. "Ludwig designed every window, door, window bar, and radiator in the noblest proportions and with such exactitude that they might have been precision instruments. Then he forged ahead with his uncompromising energy, so that everything was actually manufactured with the same exactness."[58] For instance, after the house was completely finished, he had the ceiling in one room raised by three centimeters. Though it would certainly be a mistake to interpret the architecture of the Haus Wittgenstein as the philosophy of Wittgenstein become reality—in the sense of an illustration—the exact logic of his architecture does correspond to the logical exactitude of his philosophy. Whereas in the latter half of the nineteenth century, it was ornament that was given the task of ennobling architecture, it then became the philosophically razor-sharp, well-defined architectural detail that had to take on that function. Like ornament in former times, now the detail was assigned the function of individualization and hierarchization.

VIENNA 1850–1930
ARCHITECTURE

SYNAGOGUE
(SEITENSTETTENGASSE)

JOSEF KORNHÄUSEL
1825–1826

Although the Viennese Jews, in accordance with the laws enacted under Emperor Joseph II, were allowed to build their own prayer houses, the synagogues were not permitted to appear as such in their outward aspect. They had to be "hidden" behind a "normal-looking" façade.

Josef Kornhäusel is the archetypal exponent of Viennese architecture in the first quarter of the nineteenth century, that is, of Viennese classicism and the Biedermeier. The Jewish prayer house in the Seitenstettnerhof represents the greatest artistic accomplishment in sacral architecture of this period. Since in building this synagogue Kornhäusel was not constrained to make use of any obligatory spatial canon, he created here an interior in full accord with his own artistic aims, one that proves to be a highly personal blend of stylistic principles from French Revolutionary classicism with neoclassicist/Biedermeier forms ultimately deriving from the Renaissance.

The oval, dome-vaulted interior with its columns and interposed galleries goes back to a sixteenth-century design that was already being employed for banquet halls by eighteenth-century Viennese architects. Kornhäusel himself used this spatial pattern in various forms for diverse architectural commissions.

ARSENAL, WAFFENMUSEUM
(ARSENAL, WEAPONS MUSEUM)

THEOPHIL HANSEN
1849–1856

The Weapons Museum is part of the gigantic arsenal complex, which was "to be capable of producing everything required by the Imperial and Royal Austrian Army in the way of armaments." Moreover, it was to be the central storage depot for weapons of all kinds. A competition was announced in 1849; six Viennese architects submitted plans. Each of them was entrusted with the execution of certain groups of buildings.

The Weapons Museum by Theophil Hansen is, "from an artistic standpoint, the most beautiful and richly appointed building of the Arsenal." Hansen, born in Copenhagen, lived in Athens from 1838 to 1846 and thereafter was employed in Vienna. His Weapons Museum was one of the most important works of early Viennese historicism.

It was not so much the museological presentation of the weapons collection, lauded as being "unique in all the world," which was the prime theoretical consideration, but rather the creation of an Austrian hall of fame for the glorification of the Austrian army and its commanders. Hansen's overall aim in the Weapons Museum was to produce a "magnificent monument of patriotic art" and a "grandiose creation" for Emperor Franz Joseph I.

"Das k.k. Artillerie-Arsenal zu Wien." *Allgemeine Bauzeitung* 31 (1866): 316ff.

Strobl, Alice. *Das k.k. Waffenmuseum im Arsenal. Der Bau und seine künstlerische Ausschmückung.* Vienna. Böhlau, 1961.

Wagner-Rieger, Renate, and Mara Reissberger. *Theophil Hansen.* Wiesbaden: Steiner, 1980, 38ff.

PARLAMENT
(PARLIAMENT)

THEOPHIL HANSEN
1874–1883

Whereas initial plans called for the erection of a separate building for each of the two chambers of the Austrian Parliament, it was decided in 1869, for the sake of economy, to lodge both the Upper House and the House of Representatives in one "building appropriate to the dignity of the two bodies." The parliament, kept strictly classical in form, was to become the very embodiment of the architecture of Theophil Hansen, his "most splendid creation," described as an original blend of the Greek style with that of the Renaissance.

At the heart of the whole complex is the columned hall, which may be analyzed as a temple turned inside out. What was formerly the architectural exterior became architectural interior. The purpose of this columned hall was that of a vastly monumentalized vestibule, to which were connected, at left and right, the two chambers for the deputies to the Upper House and the House of Representatives. Here, too—the chamber of the House of Representatives is still preserved in its original form—there is once again the direct connection with classical antiquity, not only in the architectonic details, but also in the sculptural and pictorial appointments.

Hansen here realized, as in no other building, his idea of the total work of art (*Gesamtkunstwerk*), the task of which was to unite sculpture and painting under the absolute sovereignty of architecture, and in which each detail, such as the banisters, was designed by the architect in his role as creative artist *par excellence*.

Das österreichische Parlament. Vienna 1984.
Wagner-Rieger, Renate, and Mara Reissberger. *Theophil von Hansen*. Wiesbaden 1980, 111ff.

Wien. 32. Neues Reichsrathsgebäude von Oberbaurath Theophil Ritter v. Hansen. Fotog. Jos. Wlha.

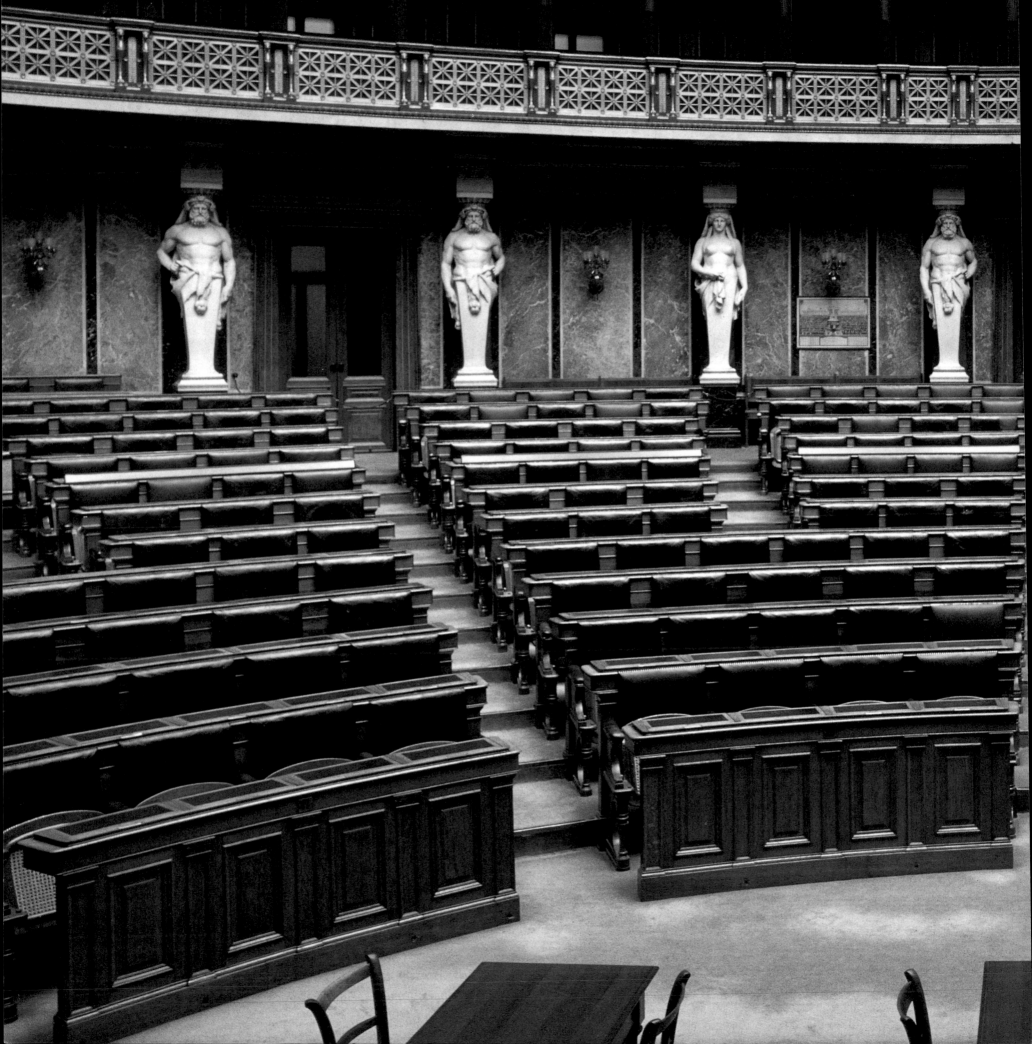

OPERA

EDUARD VAN DER NÜLL & AUGUST VON SICARDSBURG
1863–1869

The Vienna Opera was the first public monumental building to be completed on the Ringstrasse. Contemporary critics were unanimous only in respect to the quality of the interior of the Vienna Opera, "for the interior of the new operatic theater is admirable." All the more sharp, by contrast, was the criticism of the exterior architecture: it was called "the Königgrätz of architecture." (In 1866 the German troops utterly defeated the Austrian army at Königgrätz. The victory decided the Seven Weeks' War in Prussia's favor.) The main point of criticism was the architects' admixture of various stylistic models, which found expression in the following satirical quatrain: "Der Sicardsburg und van der Null, / die haben beide keinen Styl, / ob Gotik oder Renaissance, / das ist ihnen alles ans" (Roughly: Sicardsburg and van der Null, / neither one has any style, / the Gothic and the Renaissance / they use with equal complaisance). Beyond that, the architecture was accused of seeming to "sink into the terrain" instead of "rising up from the ground." The reason for this vehement contemporary critique was the shift in artistic tastes which took place at the time the Vienna Opera was built. After all, before 1870 architects had already begun to refer back to a unified stylistic model in order to transmit, with the resulting stylistic quotation, a highly specific message. Buildings became monuments to an idea. This monumentality found its expression in the high socle upon which the building came to rest. But it is just this high socle that was missing in the Vienna Opera.

The stairway and loggia, the only ostensible public spaces still preserved, were designed in the manner of the *Gesamtkunstwerk* (total work of art), of which the appointments in the loggia, with its *Magic Flute* cycle by Moritz von Schwind, represented a high-water mark.

Hoffmann, Hans-Christoph. *Walter Krause u. Werner Kitlitschka, Das Wiener Opernhaus.* Wiesbaden: Steiner, 1972.

MUSIKVEREIN
(Musical Society)

THEOPHIL HANSEN
1867–1869

Praised as the most beautiful concert hall in the world, in which the architect, Theophil Hansen, succeeded in erecting for the Gesellschaft der Musikfreunde des österreichischen Kaiserstaates (Society of the Music Lovers of the Austrian Imperial State) a "society building to grace the Imperial capital." According to contemporary assessment, Hansen created a "surprisingly rich and magnificently executed building." To the architect, the Musikverein commission offered the opportunity to distinguish himself as the builder of monumental buildings on the Ringstrasse. The loggia motif of the main façade clearly points to his artistic confrontation with the Vienna Opera. Against the anticlassical style of the Opera Hansen set the emphatic classicism of his architecture: there, the mingling of stylistic forms; here, stylistic uniformity.

The building program called for two halls, of which the larger, designed for an audience of two thousand, would also have room for roughly five hundred singers and musicians, as well as an organ. Both halls were also to be used for festivals and balls. Moreover, the building was to serve as a conservatory and, on the whole, to be "as economical as possible."

Major alterations were carried out in 1911. The grand staircases were removed, as were the statuary in the niches of the façade. The niches were replaced by windows and doors. The greatest alterations were done in the Great Hall. The caryatids that originally supported the balcony were set back against the wall, so that the balcony would jut out into the room; while this improved the lines of sight, it significantly altered the original spatial structure.

Wagner-Rieger, Renate, and Mara Reissberger. *Theophil von Hansen*. Wiesbaden: Steiner, 1980, 83ff.

KUNSTHISTORISCHES MUSEUM
(ART HISTORY MUSEUM)

GOTTFRIED SEMPER & KARL VON HASENAUER 1871–1891

The present site for the two so-called Hofmuseen (court museums)—today's Kunsthistorisches and Naturhistorisches museums—was decided upon in 1864. The plans of the four architects invited to compete for the projects were presented in 1867. Since no agreement could be reached as to which plan ought to be realized, Gottfried Semper, the German architect and architectural theoretician with the greatest worldwide reputation of the day, was called upon to take up the task. Semper did not limit himself to the question of planning the museum alone, but rather saw it as part of an overall complex. His design not only encompassed the plans for the two museums, but made them a component in a grand, overarching conception that also included the definitive extension of the Hofburg as well as a projected new Hofburg Theater. "The proud, potent magnificence of the design" was to join the "sublime temple of art" with "the splendid seat of the dynasty." In 1870 Emperor Franz Joseph I approved the realization of this *Kaiserforum*; however, it ultimately remained a torso, since the second planned wing of the Neue Hofburg was never built.

For his Viennese collaborator, Semper chose Karl von Hasenauer, to whom are attributed primarily the decorative designs for the museums, but whose influence on the overall plans ought perhaps to be rated somewhat higher. The exterior and interior design of the Kunsthistorisches Museum—whose purpose was to exalt by architectural means the artistic aura of the exhibited works of art—corresponds to the high aesthetic significance of the building.

Wagner-Rieger, Renate. *Wiens Architektur im 19. Jahrhundert*. Vienna: Bundesverlag, 1970, 175ff.
Von Vincenti, C. *Wiener Kunst-Renaissance. Studien und Charakteristiken*. Vienna: Gerold, 1876, 13ff.

BURGTHEATER

GOTTFRIED SEMPER & KARL VON HASENAUER
1874–1888

In the Burgtheater, Gottfried Semper, who originated the overall layout, further developed his architectonic concept of a theater building. The idea of having the auditorium extend outward in segments, with the stagehouse clearly demarcated, was retained in Vienna from the earlier Dresden Opera, also by Semper. New were the wings attached to the left and right; their sole function was to house the monumental and artistically magnificent stairways leading to the grand boxes. The pictorial decor of the two grand stairwells, representing the history of the theater, was carried out by the Künstlerkompagnie under the direction of the young Gustav Klimt.

The Burgtheater may be considered a typical monumental building of the Vienna Ringstrasse, one which was counted among that boulevard's most dazzling and magnificent by contemporary observers. As with the Kunsthistorisches Museum, the opulent decorative appointments originated with Karl von Hasenauer, who was also responsible for flattening the central projection facing the Ringstrasse, contrary to Semper's design.

Das neue k. k. Hofburgtheater als Bauwerk mit seinem Sculpturen—und Bilderschmuck. Vienna: Gesellschaft für vervielfältigende Kunst, 1894.

Wagner-Rieger, Renate. *Wiens Architektur im 19. Jahrhundert*. Vienna: Bundesverlag, 1970, 195ff.

Von Vincenti, C. *Wiener Kunst-Renaissance. Studien und Charakteristiken*. Vienna: Gerold, 1876, 25ff.

HAUS
SCHOT'

FELLNE

Fellner and Helmer made perh
nerships of all times. Their th
were scattered all over Europe
Budapest all the way to Ode
palaces, and villas, twenty offic
apartment houses and a consi
galleries, public baths, hospitals

One of the countless work
is Haus Sturany, designed for t
quickly risen to great weal
Ringstrasse. Not to be overlool
the aristocratic baroque palac
emphasis on the so-called *bel é*
for Viennese architecture of the
general trend. In the 1870s, the
model *par excellence*.

Hoffmann, Hans-Christoph. *Die Theaterb

PALMENHAUS
(PALM HOUSE)

FRANZ XAVER SEGENSCHMID
1879–1881

With respect both to botanical and technical considerations, the Palmenhaus at Schönbrunn may well be the most perfect establishment of its kind, providing the plant treasures, which it was designed to hold, with a home as magnificent as it is comfortable. But in stylistic and structural terms as well, it marks an interesting advance in the artistic development of iron construction; for since the past offers no model for the architectonic utilization of this modern construction material, it often appears either in the unartistic forms of practical, but unlovely, utilitarian buildings or else adopts the hypocritical mask of stone or wood construction.

Thus read a newspaper report in the year of the dedication of the Palmenhaus, in the palace gardens at Schönbrunn, the summer residence of the Austrian rulers.

The Palmenhaus is without question one of the most important iron-and-glass structures of nineteenth-century Europe, and it represents, within the exclusive group of large-scale greenhouse buildings of the nineteenth century—of which only a few examples still remain—the "crowning achievement" of that type of building. The type began with the greenhouse buildings erected in the Royal Gardens of Kew, characterized by a long hall with vaulted ceilings and a basilican schema.

What still fascinates today, as mentioned in the description cited above, is the fact that the structure is allowed to remain visible. The structure becomes the building's aesthetic quality *par excellence*.

"The overall effect creates an artistic impression whose actual cause we are at a loss to explain. It gives voice to the artistic power of the material treated in this functional manner, but we do not yet know the sources of such an impression. We are still standing at the head of a new, obscure path, on unfamiliar ground." Just a few years later, this dark path became the road to a modern, up-to-date kind of architecture.

Kohlmaier, Georg, and Barna von Sartory. *Das Glashaus. Ein Bautypus des 19. Jahrhunderts.* Munich: Prestel, 1981, 496ff. (Here, too, is the text quoted from *Illustrierte Zeitung,* 4/22/1882).

GASOMETER
(Municipal Gasworks)

STADTBAUAMT WIEN
(Municipal Building Authority of Vienna)

1893–1896

Until 1889, the job of supplying the city of Vienna with gas was entirely in the hands of private companies. In the course of the general program of communalization of the major utilities companies by the Christian Social Party under the burgomaster Karl Lueger, it was decided that contracts with the private enterprises would no longer be renewed. Therefore an international competition for a municipal gasworks was launched as early as 1892. It was won by the Berlin engineer Schimming. After several revisions, construction began under the direction of the Vienna Stadtbauamt (Municipal Building Authority) in 1896. The four gas containers that are still in existence were originally part of a more extensive complex.

These huge cylinders of fair-faced brickwork are, strictly speaking, merely the encasement for the actual gas container, the so-called bell. That which is in itself structural, technological, is here—as always in historicism—disguised, and disguised in a manner that does not permit what is hidden behind the mask to have any visual effect. What is made visible is not the structural; rather, by citing historical forms the architect awakens associations with castles and fortresses—in a romantic transfiguration, but also concealment, of modern technology. The specific aesthetic of this technical building arises precisely out of its architectonic negation of the technical.

Kortz, Paul. *Wien am Anfang des XX. Jahrhunderts. Ein Führer in technischer und künstlerischer Richtung.* Vienna: Gerlach & Wiedling, 1905, vol. 1, 241ff.

Wehdorn, Manfred, and Ute Georgeacopol-Winischhofer. *Baudenkmäler der Technik und Industrie in Österreich,* vol. 1. Vienna-Cologne-Graz: Böhlau, 1984, 54ff.

Achleitner, Friedrich. *Österreichische Architektur im 20. Jahrhundert.* vol. III/1, Salzburg-Vienna: Residenz, 1990, 304ff.

WASSERTURM
(MUNICIPAL WATER TOWER)

STADTBAUAMT WIEN
(MUNICIPAL BUILDING AUTHORITY OF VIENNA)
1898–1899

Technically, this water tower provided water to those surrounding areas that could no longer be reached using the natural pressure of the springs. It was part of a water-pumping station. Water was pumped from a container to the water tower, which was situated at the highest point in the area; from there, the high parts of the district could be supplied with water.

Architecturally, the water tower provided a landmark for this outer district of Vienna, and not only because of its exposed position on the crest of the Wienerberg. The exterior design contributed greatly to this identifying function. Here too, though, the technological and structural were disguised by the architectonic covering, which transformed the engineered necessity of this building into something seemingly useless, a romanticized garden architecture, a lookout tower. In fact, even today it is seen as the particular, and praiseworthy, characteristic of this water tower that it offers "one of the finest scenic views in Vienna." The functionally significant element is transformed by the historicist "garment" into something that can be appreciated, in terms of aesthetics, only as being without purpose. Or, to put it differently: the builders took care not to confront the viewer of this architecture with the naked functionalism of the engineered building, but rather designed it, so to speak, as experiential architecture.

Kortz, Paul. *Wien am Anfang des XX. Jahrhunderts. Ein Führer in technischer und künstlerischer Richtung.* Vienna: Gerlach & Wiedling 1905, vol. 1, 238ff.

Wehdorn, Manfred, and Ute Georgeacopol-Winischhofer. *Baudenkmäler der Technik und Industrie in Österreich,* vol. 1. Vienna-Cologne-Graz: Böhlau, 1984, 54ff.

LÄNDERBANK

OTTO WAGNER
1882–1884

"The Länderbank is proof of genius from the early phase," said J. A. Lux in the monograph on Otto Wagner that appeared during the artist's lifetime. The Länderbank is among Wagner's earlier works, in which he made unmistakable recourse to historical models. As in all of his works from this period, he engaged the architecture of the Renaissance. This adoption of the Renaissance is made evident both in the façade and the interior, with the ecclesiastical character of the space endowing this particular building, devoted to profane monetary transactions, with an air of consecration.

Disregarding for the moment the sacral nature of the interior, which would predominate in the Postsparkasse (Postal Savings Bank) twenty years later, it was above all the solution for the floor plan that elicited the prompt admiration of Wagner's contemporaries. Confronting an extremely irregular building site, Wagner displaced the axial kink resulting from the ground plan's odd configuration into a central, circular vestibule, thus making it imperceptible. In this manner, the break in the axial sequence of the rooms was made to disappear. "Whoever, coming in from the street, wishes to enter the main hall, where customer transactions are conducted, proceeds first of all, via a few stairs, into a circular hall, a kind of vestibule. From there the path leads directly to the main hall. There is no searching, no fumbling, no going wrong; one has the sensation of being able to advance straight ahead by the simplest and easiest path to the tellers' counters. One does not even notice that the axis of the building makes a bend here, one which could otherwise easily disorient the visitor and evoke an impression of being crooked and contrary to sense. An amazingly simple solution, one that is for that very reason ingenious."

Lux, Joseph August. *Otto Wagner. Eine Monographie.* Munich: Delphin, 1914, 57ff.

BRIDGE, WIENZEILE

OTTO WAGNER
1896–1898

In 1890 it was decided that the outlying districts of Vienna should be incorporated into the actual municipality. This act necessitated not only a "general regulation plan" for Vienna, but also the construction of new public transportation facilities. One important project that resulted was the so-called Vienna Stadtbahn, or urban rail system, planned to be both a subway and an elevated rail. In 1894 Otto Wagner was recruited as the artistic director of the plan, which was already moving ahead at full speed. In existence at this time was "no more nor less than a completely worked-out plan," one that called for an architectonic design using the rough brickwork "taken stylistically from the common Gothic forms" which had been current "for decades in railway construction and civil engineering in general." The contract drawn up with Wagner in 1894 guaranteed the architect the right to architectural design in accord with his artistic principles. "To him belongs the credit for having designed the facilities of the Stadtbahn to be both artistically beautiful and practically modern. No railway station, no depot, no viaduct arch, no bridge was permitted to be contracted out that had not been designed in an artistic and modern manner in Wagner's studio. The stone masses and iron structures first had to be put into forms pleasing to the eye and not affronting to the aesthetic sense."

Among all the bridges built for the Vienna Stadtbahn, the enormous span erected over the Wienzeile occupies a special position. Wagner designed it to resemble a monumental city gate, thus accentuating the boundary between the central part of Vienna and the former suburbs. With the permeability of his Stadtbahn architecture, however, Wagner simultaneously dramatized this problem: the lines drawn by the Stadtbahn actually had here the exclusionary character of an architectonically reformulated city wall. In his artistic conception, Wagner accentuated the dialectic between the aesthetic-architectonic design of the bridge piers and the technical aesthetic of the iron structure, which purported to result solely from necessity.

Kolb, Günter. *Otto Wagner und die Wiener Stadtbahn*. Munich: Scaneg, 1989, 213ff.

HOFPAVILLON HIETZING
(COURT PAVILION AT HIETZING)

OTTO WAGNER
1897–1899

In the course of planning the individual stations for the Wiental (Vienna valley) stretch of the Vienna Stadtbahn, the idea was first raised in 1896 of building a special "Waiting Room for the Most High Court" close to the Hietzing station, in the immediate vicinity of the summer palace at Schönbrunn. It was to serve the emperor, the members of the court, and "crowned heads" visiting Vienna as a convenient spot for entering and exiting the Vienna Stadtbahn network. Approved in 1897, the definitive plans were ready by 1898. Sources show that the emperor used the Court Pavilion exactly twice, both times for the dedication ceremonies for a section of the Vienna Stadtbahn.

In creating the Court Pavilion, Wagner succeeded—at least this one time—in fulfilling his dream of acting as architect to the imperial family. None of his other projects for the Hapsburgs, such as the expansion of the Hofburg and the redesign of the imperial burial chapel, were ever realized.

It was expressly requested that the architecture of the Court Pavilion be brought into "harmony with the style of the Schönbrunn pleasure palace." This explains the rather baroque tenor of Wagner's design, which stands in contrast to the more distinctly classical architecture of many of his other Stadtbahn stations. "The heart of the building is the imperial waiting salon. It has an octagonal floor plan and is crowned by a chased copper cupola. It is remarkable how the latter produces a pleasant link with the baroque buildings of Schönbrunn Palace, though naturally without copying a single baroque form."

Much was made of the way in which Wagner, particularly in the interior, took into account the building's function. In order to "shorten the seconds spent waiting by the monarch with the sight of a work of art, Wagner made room in his plans for an art work, but one which also served a purpose, namely that of" allowing the emperor to visually survey "the entire expanse of the new Stadtbahn facilities in the bird's-eye view of Vienna painted by Carl Moll." The carpet, too, bore not just any pattern, but was "actually decorated with the paths that the emperor [could] take upon exiting through any of the various doors of the room."

"Der Hofpavillon der Wiener Stadtbahn." In *Ver Sacrum II* 8 (1899): 3ff.
Otto Wagner, Stadtbahnstation-Hofpavillon Hietzing. Vienna: Historisches Museum der Stadt Wien, 1990.

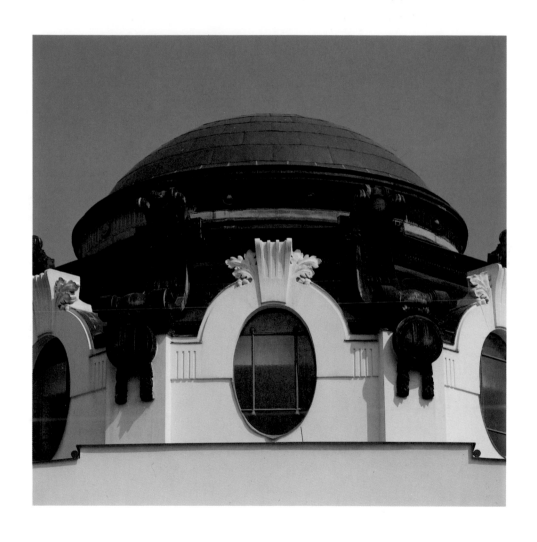

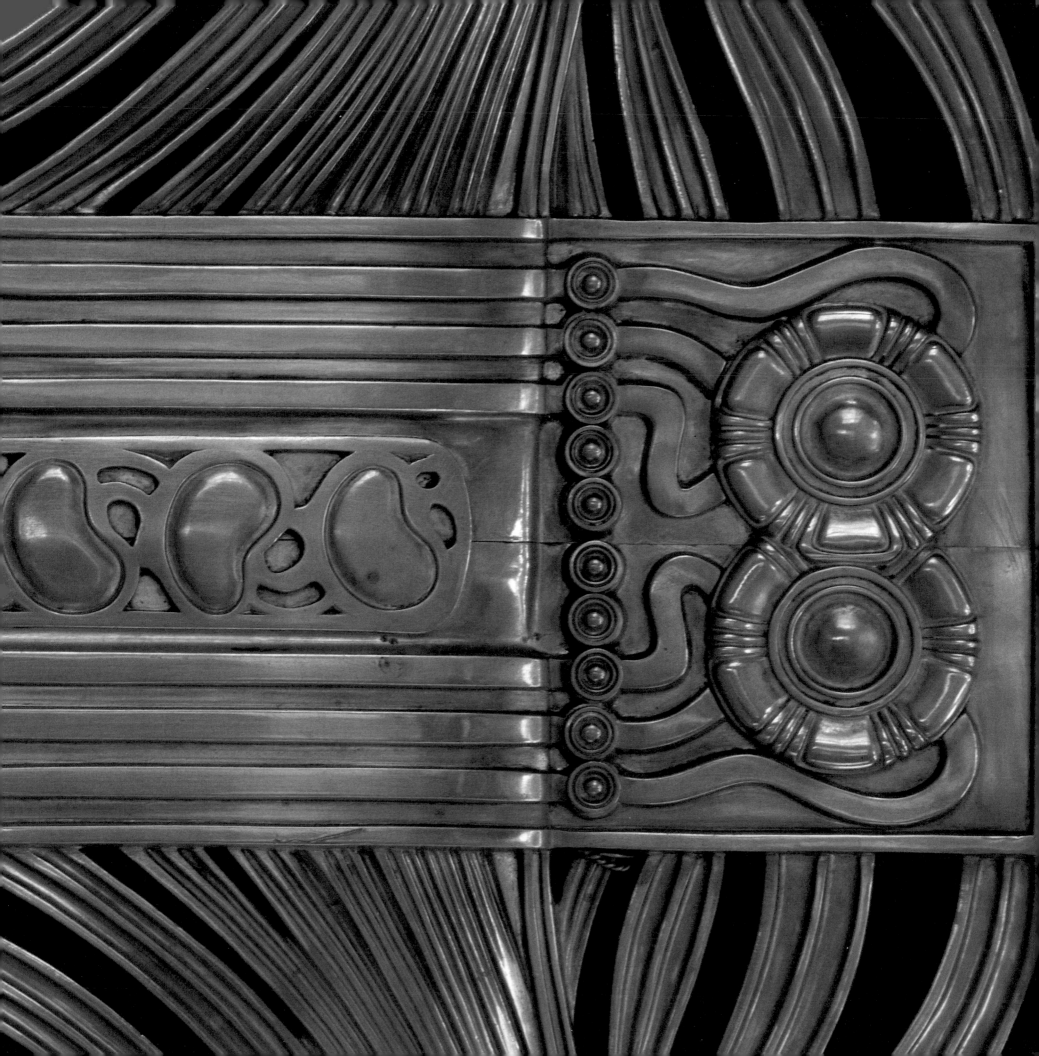

STATION KARLSPLATZ
(KARLSPLATZ STATION)

OTTO WAGNER
1898–1899

"Delicate, light forms of polished, white marble, iron and Secession-green decor"—so Ludwig Hevesi, the hagiographer of incipient Viennese modernism, described the Stadtbahn pavilions on the Karlsplatz by Otto Wagner, which he called "masterpieces in their own way." Unlike all of his other stations, Wagner's plans for the Karlsplatz facility call for two entrance pavilions facing each other. These, in effect, mark the intersection of the elongated axis of the Karlskirche with the axis of the street leading to the Ringstrasse (the Akademiestrasse)—while simultaneously concealing the axial break.

Stylistically, the Karlsplatz pavilions—and the Majolikahaus—belong to Wagner's short, transitional Jugendstil phase, a phase in which he was much influenced by his pupils, to a great extent leaving to them the details of design and above all the outward appearance of his buildings. The sunflower ornamentation of the pavilions, for instance, originated with J. M. Olbrich, the builder of the Secession. For Wagner himself, this Jugendstil phase remained a brief episode, after he had broken with the neo-Renaissance of his early period but was still in search of a new, independent style of his own, such as was demonstrated in the buildings erected after 1900, the Postsparkasse (Postal Savings Bank) and the Kirche am Steinhof (Steinhof Church).

The structure of the pavilions already points to the style of the later Wagner. Thin marble slabs are hung upon an iron framework; all the while, the structural scaffolding remains visible, an essential contribution to the aesthetic design. Thus he gave visible, architectural expression to his motto *Artis sola domina necessitas* (Necessity alone is the mistress of art), and to his view that structure is the "primordial cell of architecture, for without it no art form can arise."

Kolb, Günter. *Otto Wagner und die Wiener Stadtbahn*. Munich: Scaneg, 1989, 310ff.

BUILDINGS AT LINKE WIENZEILE 38 & 40

OTTO WAGNER
1898–1899

In 1898 and 1899, at the corner of Linke Wienzeile and Köstlergasse, Otto Wagner erected an ensemble consisting of three apartment buildings. As in previous enterprises, and later again with the apartment buildings at Neustiftgasse—Döblergasse, here too he was at once the buildings' owner and architect; that is, he bought the construction site, erected the buildings, and sold them upon completion. Acting as his own client, he was in this way best able to realize his latest ideas for a contemporary apartment building.

Since the 1890s, Wagner had been propagating his idea of turning the Wienzeile into a grand boulevard connecting the Hofburg (the imperial seat) with Schönbrunn (the emperor's summer residence). In keeping with this, he designed his buildings on the Wienzeile to be appropriately opulent and architecturally attractive. In the corner building, most critical from an urban architect's point of view, Wagner's powers of architectonic design are concentrated on the corner solution and on the front facing the Wienzeile. Gold, the precious material *par excellence*, is here employed in decoratively ennobling the façade. It is not the quantity of the chosen ornamental form that matters, but rather its quality, its material value. The two figures in the roof area were intended to proclaim to all the world the new, innovative nature of Wagner's architecture.

The façade of the building at Linke Wienzeile 40 was determined by quite different considerations. Wagner clad the entire living area of the building with majolica tiles, which, in the aggregate, cover the façade with a decorative floral pattern. With this tile cladding, Wagner followed his own reflections on practicality and usefulness; in his opinion such a façade cladding possessed the extremely desirable quality of being, so to speak, indestructible. Furthermore, it needed only simple washing to make it look like new. In this manner he wishes to prove that satisfying modern requirements did not mean that one must necessarily give up aesthetic exaltation.

Asenbaum, Paul, Peter Haiko, et al. *Otto Wagner. Möbel und Innenräume*. Salzburg-Vienna: Residenz, 1984.

POSTSPARKASSE
(POSTAL SAVINGS BANK)

OTTO WAGNER 1904–1907
(ANNEX 1910–1912)

The Postsparkasse (Postal Savings Bank) and the Kirche am Steinhof (Steinhof Church), created simultaneously, represent the high-water mark in the architectural career of Otto Wagner. "Nothing in the Postal Savings Bank in the least recalls the 'free Renaissance.' No reminiscence of historical styles, no palazzo architecture, no monumentality out of the treasure-chamber of tradition—instead all is functional. Questions of material come to the fore. Ferroconcrete, glass, marble, aluminum, vulcanite, and so on, are the elements of which the work is composed. At the time the Länderbank was built, no architect would ever have thought of these. Otto Wagner discovered them. Although he did not actually invent these materials, he was the one who invested them with their current significance; he discovered their practical utility for architecture." To this modernity in the materials corresponded the modern element in his architectural design, both exterior and interior.

Wagner clad the entire façade with very thin marble slabs, thus considerably abbreviating—compared with other monumental buildings on the Vienna Ringstrasse—the required construction time, while still achieving, in his opinion, a greater monumentality. The function of the overly conspicuous bolts is to point unmistakably to this cladding of the façade.

The glass-iron structure of the main hall emphasizes the technoid element without neglecting the aesthetic. It is precisely those utterly technological aspects that ostensibly create the new artistic-aesthetic form. Over and over, Wagner put "functional" necessity emphatically in the foreground. The way they were conceived, for instance, the warm-air blowers lost their purely utilitarian function, becoming self-sufficient works of art, sculptures. Thus, the necessary did not retain its utilitarian form, but rather received its own aura as an art form. The aura, in this process of transformation, was given the task of aesthetically exalting the practical value of the object, thus making of it a work of art and ritual.

Asenbaum, Paul, Peter Haiko, et al. *Otto Wagner. Möbel und Innenräume.* Salzburg-Vienna: Residenz, 1984.

KIRCHE AM STEINHOF
(STEINHOF CHURCH)

OTTO WAGNER
1904–1907

The Kirche am Steinhof (Steinhof Church) is the crowning glory of the "State Sanatorium and Home for the Mentally and Neurologically Ill 'Am Steinhof,'" begun in 1901. Engaged to build what was, at that time, the "most modern" asylum in Europe was the most modern architect in Vienna, who proceeded to build a truly modern church.

In the Kirche am Steinhof, Otto Wagner realized his reflections on "modernism in church architecture" and the "architecture of our times." True to his motto "All modern creations must meet the requirements of the present if they are to be fit for modern humanity," he designed the up-to-date ecclesiastical building: the interior bright and unsupported, the façade clad in thin marble slabs. "Whoever believes that the mystical-religious impulse within us is fostered in the semidarkness of badly ventilated, dank, cold church rooms will find this notion brilliantly refuted by Wagner. A blessed cheerfulness flows about the visitor and leads him into devout meditation that knows more of joy than of fear." To some not-so-well-meaning contemporary critics, by contrast, the church gave anything but the impression of a Christian house of God. One of them even compared it with the "tomb of an Indian maharajah."

Wagner paid special attention to the Steinhof Church's function as a sanatorium chapel for the mentally ill. The uppermost concern was for cleanliness and hygiene, as well as for the need, in case of a seizure, for example, to be able to assist the patients at once. This was the reason for the extremely short pews, the original construction of the holy-water fonts (to prevent infections), the floor that slopes gently toward the altar and was thus easy to clean.

Wagner's preeminent architectural quality lies in the fact that, despite all these practical considerations, he never neglected beauty. With the *Gesamtkunstwerk* (total work of art) that is the Steinhof Church, he intended to prove his idea that the practical can also be beautiful the reverse, as it were, of his axiom "The impractical can never be beautiful."

Haiko, Peter, Harald Leupold-Löwenthal, and Mara Reissberger. "Die weisse Stadt—Der Steinhof in Wien. Architektur als Reflex der Einstellung zur Geisteskrankheit." In *kritische berichte,* vol. 9, 1981, nr. 6, S. 3ff. (Published in English under the title "The White City—The Steinhof in Vienna. Architecture as a Reflection of the Attitude toward Mental Illness." In *Sigmund Freud House Bulletin,* vol. 5, no. 2, 1981, 10ff).

APARTMENT BUILDINGS AT NEUSTIFTGASSE 40— DÖBLERGASSE 4

OTTO WAGNER 1909–1912

Otto Wagner erected the corner house at Neustiftgasse 40 between 1909 and 1911, followed by the adjacent apartment building at Döblergasse 4 from 1911 to 1912. As with the group of buildings at Linke Wienzeile, Wagner built these two apartment buildings at his own expense, and thus was, once again, his own client.

Even more conspicuously than in the Wienzeile buildings, the exterior was made to express Wagner's concept of the modern apartment building as a "cell conglomerate." Floor after floor, the windows are all aligned along the same formulaic axes. The "uniformity of apartment buildings" mentioned by Wagner was the result of "the lifestyles of the people, which daily grow more similar." As far as outward appearance was concerned, he found, "Since the rental value of the individual floors has been nearly equalized by the addition of passenger elevators, the natural consequence had to be that the differentiation of the floors by outward artistic design was no longer advisable. Architectonic designs that seek their motifs in palace architecture must therefore be considered entirely misplaced in such cell conglomerates, simply because they contradict the inner structure of the building." Hence, "in designing the façade of the modern apartment building, the architect is thrown back upon a smooth surface interrupted by many windows of equal value, to which is added the protective principal cornice and at most a crowning frieze and a portal."

As a new kind of "decor," the address of the building itself, "Neustiftgasse 40," appeared in enormous letters. In doing this, Wagner once again followed his basic principle, namely, that any kind of decoration, any ornament, must be founded in functionality. The functional, the utilitarian thus became the aesthetic, the beautiful. The utilitarian style that Wagner propagated was actually the style of useful beauty. The beautiful was, simultaneously, useful.

Wagner, Otto. *Die Baukunst unserer Zeit* (4th edition of *Moderne Architektur.*) Vienna: Schroll, 1914, 86ff. New edition, Vienna: Löcker, 1979.
Asenbaum, Paul, Peter Haiko, et al. *Otto Wagner. Möbel und Innenräume.* Salzburg-Vienna: Residenz, 1984.

SECESSION
(Secession Building)

J. M. OLBRICH
1897–1898

In 1897 the Vienna Secession, whose official name was Vereinigung bildender Künstler Österreichs (Austrian Association of Fine Artists), split off from the old Genossenschaft bildender Künstler Wiens (Viennese Cooperative of Fine Artists). Among the most important founding members were Gustav Klimt, Carl Moll, Joseph Maria Olbrich, and Koloman Moser. Their goal was to combat "backwardness in art" and to strive for reform in the way exhibitions were customarily run. It was plain that the "hearth of the newly ignited fire" must be "our own exhibition hall," whose design was undertaken by J. M. Olbrich.

Olbrich's architecture set itself apart, in programmatic fashion, from the historicist architecture current in Vienna at that time. Set against the pragmatism of which historicism stood accused was the holy flame of artistic creativity. Olbrich recalled, "With what joy did I give birth to this building! Out of a chaos of ideas, an enigmatic tangle of emotional stances, a jumble of good and evil it sprouted, not easily! Walls were to come into being, white and shining, holy and chaste. Earnest dignity was to weave about it all. Pure dignity." Critics, by contrast, called the building a "hybrid born of temple and magazine" and found fault with "the Asiatic uncouthness of this silhouette." For them, the architecture of the Secession building did not "find a new architectonic formula," but rather was ruled by "mere decorative inspirations." Also objected to was the manifold symbolism contained within the architecture, because the building was "more cerebrally poetic than structurally architectonic," and because—in the opinion of the critics—"every architectonic truthfulness is sacrificed" to it.

The most important thing, not only in an architectural-formal sense but also in terms of symbolic content, was the partially gilded semidome of laurel leaves. The evergreen laurel was seen as the symbol of victory, peace, immortality, and dignity; healing and purifying powers were also ascribed to it. The snake motif occurring here stood for metamorphosis, renewal, and transcendence.

Kapfinger, Otto, and Adolf Krischanitz. *Die Wiener Secession. Das Haus—Entstehung, Geschichte, Erneuerung.* Vienna-Cologne-Graz: Böhlau, 1986.

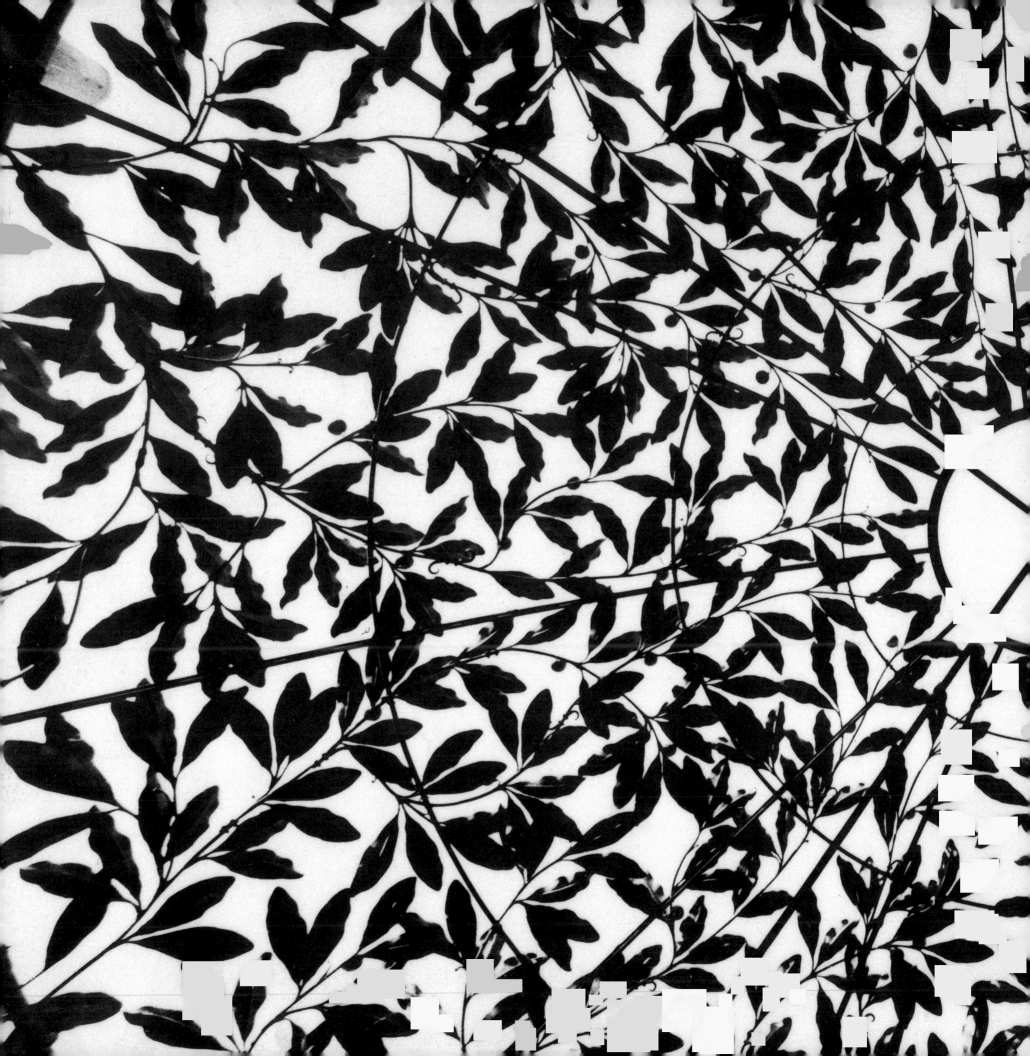

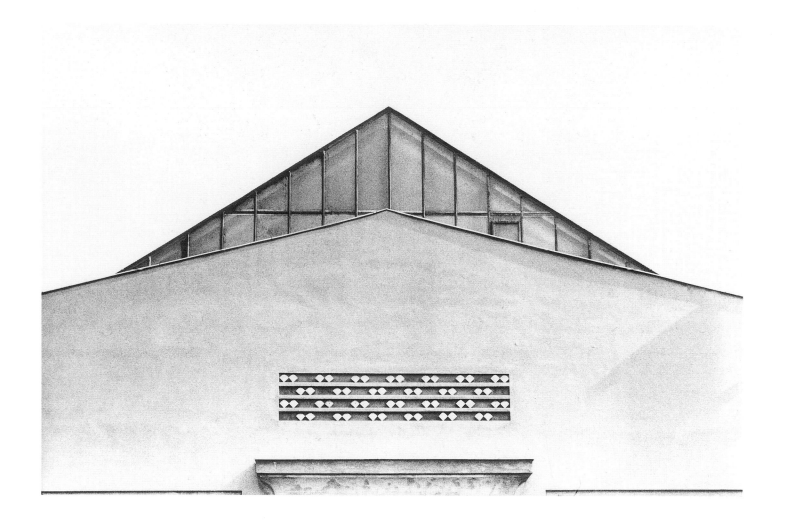

PORTOIS & FIX BUILDING

MAX FABIANI
1899–1900

Ludwig Hevesi said of the Portois and Fix building: "These leading purveyors of furniture have recently opened their new business premises in the Ungargasse. The building was designed by the architect Max Fabiani and makes a big impression with its imposing, highly modern façade. The first two floors are shop space with show windows and are clad on the outside in two shades of polished Swedish granite. The three floors above are covered in rectangular slabs of pyrogranite, in various shades and tones of bright green and brown (from the ceramics workshop of Szolnay in Fünfkirchen). The effect of the rock-solid, lustrous material is superb; what is more, the effect is entirely undisturbed, since any conventional organization or segmentation (of the surface) has been avoided. Acting as decoration for the façade, by the way, is a series of eight metallic lamp holders that sprout from the wall surface in stately curves, bearing arc lamps. The top story, too, constructed of glass and iron to serve as a studio, is furnished with a row of iron braces that add to the decorative effect."

Before building the Portois & Fix building, Max Fabiani spent two years in the studio of Otto Wagner. The latter's influence on the Portois & Fix building is unmistakable. The cladding of the façade with slabs finds its direct precursor in the Majolikahaus. Fabiani, however, gave his building a geometric ornamental pattern, emphasizing by means of this decorative abstraction the additive nature of the façade's composition. It is remarked that, on the whole, Fabiani has here "carried out the teachings of the 'Wagner school' he so zealously champions with the uttermost consistency."

Hevesi, Ludwig. In *Kunst und Kunsthandwerk* 4 (1901): 321ff.
Die Architektur des XX. Jahrhunderts, vol. 3, 1903, no. 37 (Reprinted in English: Peter Haiko, comp. *Architecture of the Early XX Century.* New York: Rizzoli, 1989).
Pozzetto, Marco. *Max Fabiani. Ein Architect der Monarchie.* Vienna: Tusch, 1983, 63ff.

ARTARIA
BUILDING

MAX FABIANI
1900–1901

Ludwig Hevesi called the Artaria Building a "highly modern new building that causes much stopping and staring among passersby. . .a real child of its times, one that wouldn't think of presenting itself as anything older and loftier." "The principles of functionality and genuineness have here become flesh and bone, that is to say, marble and iron." The building is primarily designed for business use, "although the upper floors are set up as living quarters."

The cladding of the façade in marble, as propagated by Otto Wagner, was here made a reality by Fabiani—and this was several years before Wagner himself was able to do so in his Postsparkasse (Postal Savings Bank) and Kirche am Steinhof (Steinhof Church). The use of bolts to fasten the slabs was also anticipated here. But whereas Wagner always had monumental buildings in mind for his façades clad in marble slabs, Fabiani here used them for a private building, thus achieving, with contemporary means, a monumentalization of the business premises for the "venerable art firm of Artaria & Co." Particularly noticeable are the windows, which project beyond the surface of the façade—a feature doubtless patterned after English models.

The four pillars of the socle zone, clad in red Hungarian marble, visibly support iron girders. With this effect Fabiani not only demonstratively put the classical building material, marble, in direct contact with the modern material, iron, but also the classical element of support with the modern method of bearing loads.

Hevesi, Ludwig. In *Kunst und Kunsthandwerk* 5 (1902): 273.

Pozzetto, Marco. *Max Fabiani. Ein Architekt der Monarchie*. Vienna: Tusch, 1983, 76ff.

ZACHERL BUILDING

JOSEF PLECNIK
1903–1905

In 1900 Johann E. Zacherl, whose wealth was founded upon the production of an organic insect pesticide, turned to Otto Wagner for sound suggestions about the new business premises and dwelling that he proposed to build. Wagner held an internal competition among his students, which was won by Josef Plecnik. Although Plecnik's competition design of 1900 must be seen as a direct engagement of Wagner's Majolikahaus on the Wienzeile, in his executed version of 1903 Plecnik arrived at an architectonic solution that demonstrated a treatment highly independent of Wagner's ideas.

Plecnik covered the façade with granite slabs, thus adopting Wagner's programmatic cladding theory; but in his choice of a specific material he set himself decidedly apart from Wagner. In place of the color white, with its air of the clinically hygienic, he selected the more somber and mystical gray. Plecnik responded to the supposed rationality of the Vienna Secession and incipient Viennese modernism with an architecture that some contemporaries felt to be poetic. The Viennese coffee-house author Peter Altenberg said, "Indescribable was the impression [made by] this noble, simple and yet mysterious palace of the gods, [this] modern, livable Valhalla, in the midst of those thousands of cardboard-covered tenements. Proportioned like basalt cliffs, and with steep walls, it seemed to me like a tragic grandiose poetry."

Compared, for instance, with Wagner's Postsparkasse (Postal Savings Bank), Plecnik also developed an autonomous way of fastening the granite slabs. He sets round rod moldings in the joints between the individual slabs; these in fact not only held the slabs in place, but also lent rhythm to the façade, owing to the alternation of wider and narrower slabs. To Wagner's strictly rational additive series, Plecnik counterposes a suspenseful, modulated articulation of the façade.

"But wait until you see the vestibule and the stairwell in the Zacherl house! Once you do you are sure to be in ecstasy!" The vestibule, in the archaic-classical manner of a columned hall, the oval stairwell with its candelabra—all of this reveals Plecnik's enormous fecundity of form. Having abandoned the rationality of the Wagner school, he betrayed, in his complexity and contradictions, a uniquely mannerist pose.

Prelovsek, Damjan. *Josef Plecnik. Wiener Arbeiten von 1896 bis 1914.* Vienna: Tusch. 1979, 81ff.

HEILIGGEIST KIRCHE
(HOLY SPIRIT CHURCH)

JOSEF PLECNIK
1910–1913

Josef Plecnik played here—with ironic distance—with the vocabulary of classical forms and architecture. In the main façade he unmistakably quoted a temple front from classical antiquity; in the interior as well he unmistakably quoted the quintessential Christian ecclesiastical architecture, namely the basilica. The use of ferroconcrete building techniques permitted him a free, unforced dialogue with the architectural past. The interior, in a complex contradiction, can be interpreted as a hall room with galleries suspended at the sides; but at the same time as a basilica, one in which the division, by means of supports, into nave and accompanying side aisles has disappeared. No architectonic elements, such as columns or pillars, bear the high wall of the nave; of the wall itself only a vestige remains, and the supports in the gallery zone visually reduce their original function to absurdity, since they can only be interpreted as the means of suspension of the galleries, not as the elements that uphold the ceiling.

Whereas Plecnik used ferroconcrete in the upper portion of the church in order to achieve precisely this kind of reinterpretation of traditional ecclesiastical forms, he demonstrated in the crypt the expressive possibilities inherent in the new material, and the high degree of expressivity achieved in architecture.

The imperial heir apparent, Archduke Franz Ferdinand—who, in the years leading up to his assassination and the end of the Hapsburg monarchy, was responsible for all artistic issues of the realm—was known for his extremely conservative taste in art, and was notorious among the modernists. If he found, upon completion of Wagner's Steinhof Church, that he preferred the "style of Maria Theresa" (i.e., the neo-Baroque), his reaction to Plecnik's church was still more caustic. He called it a mixture "of a temple to Venus, a Russian bath, and a stable or hayloft."

Prelovsek, Damjan. *Josef Plecnik. Wiener Arbeiten von 1896 bis 1914*. Vienna: Tusch, 1979, 145ff.

ABSCHLUß DER WIENFLUßEINWÖLBUNG
(ARCH OVER THE RIVER WIEN)

FRIEDRICH OHMANN & JOSEF HACKHOFER 1903–1906

Beginning in 1904, Friedrich Ohmann, primarily active in Prague and Vienna, held master classes in architecture alongside those of Otto Wagner at the Vienna Academy of Fine Arts. He represented what may be termed the more traditional, extremely moderate modernist faction in *fin-de-siècle* Viennese architecture. Just as Otto Wagner was assigned the artistic design of the Stadtbahn facilities, so Friedrich Ohmann was entrusted with the regulation and arch over the river Wien. Special significance was attached to the point where the Wien flowed into the grounds of the Stadtpark (municipal park). Ohmann's project called for a baroque, illusionist architecture of portals and pavilions, with promenades along the banks, sets of stairs, water basins, fountains, semicircular niches, resting places, landings, fabulous gargoyles, mermaids, and so on. As a whole, however, the project remained a torso, especially in respect to the sculptural decoration. Never realized, in particular, was Ohmann's "practical" idea of preventing the escape of foul odors from the subterranean section of the Wien by means of a curtain of water.

Ohmann's theme was not the technological "taming" of nature, which, after all, is what the regulation of any stream or river is about. Just the opposite was true: Ohmann's subject was the romantic merging of architecture and nature. In his conception, the organic and the manufactured entered into an indissoluble symbiosis. The plants called for by the original concept were to be architecturalized; the architecture and its inseparable sculpture showed, in part, organic characteristics. But this spoke to essential elements of the Jugendstil.

Von Feldegg, Ferdinand. *Friedrich Ohmann's Entwürfe und ausgeführte Bauten. Mit einem Anhange von Studien.* Vienna: Schroll, 1906.
Pötzl-Malikova, Maris. *Die Plastik der Ringstrasse 1890–1918.* Wiesbaden: Steiner, 1976, 37ff.

SANATORIUM PURKERSDORF

JOSEF HOFFMANN 1904

"That is Josef Hoffmann. That is the moving spirit behind the 'Wiener Werkstätte.' The drab box that most others would have set in place, with an eye to the restrictions imposed by a building designed to be profitable, becomes, in his hand, a meaningful form in which one immediately detects the logical organism. No braggadocio of false ornament, of columns and gables, no tricks of various colors disturb the simple harmony of this building executed in light-colored, roughcast plasterwork. Only a narrow decorative strip of white and blue square tiles sets off all the edges and surrounds every window." The sanatorium was conceived as a health resort for well-to-do patients and was meant to satisfy the highest standards with regard to comfort and luxury. Ludwig Hevesi, the chronicler of Viennese modernism, explicitly thought of "ladies in full evening dress swishing up the stairs to the dining hall."

The exterior is characterized by a clearly defined sculptural modeling, with individual structural members now projecting, now receding. In complex contradiction to this is the emphatic planarity, taken by itself, of each of the façade's components. This is the result of Josef Hoffmann's framing of all surfaces and openings with a narrow strip of white and blue square tiles (something one encounters with time and again in his work), as well as the lack of any kind of architectonic elements of spatial organization.

"A walk through the rooms of this building is exceedingly stimulating. One sees nothing but new, newer, newest. Hoffmann's fertile powers of invention easily pour forth every imaginable convenience and functional amenity, both small and large; and a sketch from his hand is enough for the well-schooled employees of the 'Wiener Werkstätte,' that elite among the artisans of Vienna, to turn his thoughts into action. Not only 'every nail,' as the saying goes, has been devised by him, but also every border for the furniture fabrics invented by him is woven according to his drawings. He quite simply thinks of everything."

In 1926 one story was added to the building, thus altering its original character.

Hevesi, Ludwig. "Neubauten von Josef Hoffmann." In *Altkunst—Neukunst. Wien 1894–1908.* Vienna: Konegen, 1909, 214ff.

Sekler, Eduard F. *Josef Hoffmann. Das architektonische Werk. Monographie und Werkverzeichnis.* Salzburg-Vienna: Residenz, 1982.

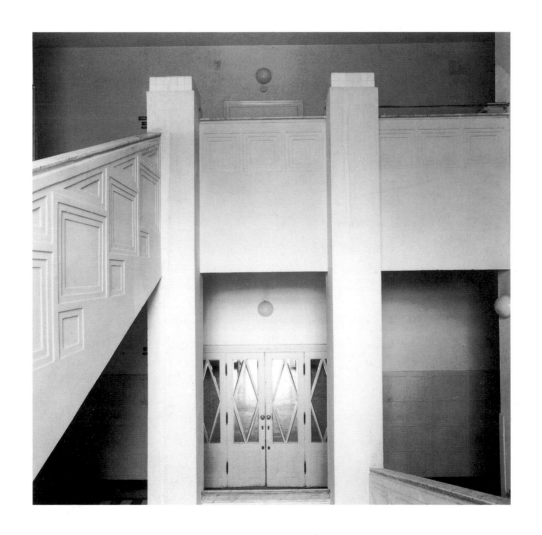

VILLA SKYWA-PRIMAVESI

JOSEF HOFFMANN
1913–1915

Apart from the Palais Stoclet in Brussels, also by Josef Hoffmann, the Skywa-Primavesi house is probably one of the most lavish and ostentatious of the villas he built. Robert Primavesi, major landowner, big industrialist, and a representative in parliament, had the building erected for Josefine Skywa, "a companion of his later years." To the overall complex belong, in addition to the actual house, a greenhouse, a garage with a porter's lodge, and the so-called Teetempelchen (little tea temple) with a pond and pergola.

Characteristic of the exterior is the unmistakable classicism, typical of Josef Hoffmann's style from 1910 on. Fluted pillars and triangular pediments with sculptured figures are the essential elements of this neoclassicism. Of no less significance is the additive joining together of distinct architectural bodies, with each building component defining a specific living area. The monumentalized design of the exterior finds its exact correspondence in that of the interior. With the high, marble-clad stairway hall and the large central hall with its stairs to the upper story, the public sphere of the villa is over-explicitly accentuated.

Here, again, Hoffmann's intention to create a *Gesamtkunstwerk* (total work of art) determined the design; but in this instance that same tendency also encompasses the surrounding garden.

Sekler, Eduard F. *Josef Hoffmann. Das architektonische Werk. Monographie und Werkverzeichnis.* Salzburg-Vienna: Residenz, 1982.

VILLA KNIPS

JOSEF HOFFMANN
1924–1925

The Knips house is the last in the series of large urban villas built by Josef Hoffmann. In contrast to Villa Skywa-Primavesi, the classicist tenor of this architecture is subdued; what stands out here is rather the Viennese variant on the more private Biedermeier style. Hoffmann fell back on the traditional form of the closed solidium, yet he emphasized not the mass per se, but each individual delimiting surface. Façade after façade appears as an almost immaterial, thin surface, which Hoffmann joined at the edges with the next surface. The small, diamond-shaped decorative elements on the façade represent a recollection of his teacher, Otto Wagner; they are a playful paraphrase of Wagner's bolts on the Postsparkasse (Postal Savings Bank) and the Kirche am Steinhof (Steinhof Church). Here, however, they have irrevocably reverted to being purely functionless decoration.

In the interior, too, the return to the Biedermeier is predominant, although mixed with typical Art Deco forms. And here, again, Josef Hoffmann's will to design dominated each and every thing; even the partition separating living hall from dining room and kitchen from pantry, with wall-high glass cabinets on either side, originated with him.

As a whole, Villa Knips is—apart from the Palais Stoclet—at the present time probably the best preserved example of the decorative art of Josef Hoffmann.

Sekler, Eduard F. *Josef Hoffmann. Das architektonische Werk. Monographie und Werkverzeichnis.* Salzburg-Vienna: Residenz, 1982.

HAUS AM MICHAELERPLATZ
(BUILDING ON THE MICHAELERPLATZ)

ADOLF LOOS 1910–1912

This work was commissioned by the tailoring firm of Goldman & Salatsch; plans called for both business premises and living quarters. (Besides the actual sales area, the business section also encompassed a mezzanine gallery for the tailor's shop.) Although in his original plans Loos proposed a thoroughly conventional façade design—perhaps so as not to delay the necessary building permits—in the next planning phase he curtailed the amount of ornamentation, and, in the final version—in keeping with his principles—did away with decoration altogether. Whereupon, by order of the Stadtbauamt (municipal building authority), construction was called to a halt. A competition was arranged to come up with an after-the-fact design for the "naked" façade. Loos protested, the jury resigned, and the idea of the competition was abandoned. The flower boxes that were finally installed represented a compromise between Adolf Loos and the authorities. Loos himself had this to say about the conflict: "A curious case for the architectural chronicles of Vienna. Work on the façade of a new building was officially forbidden as a conflict had arisen between the architect of the building and the municipal building authority, not because the architect lavished too much of his art on the building, but rather, and this is the novelty, because he wanted to apply too little ornament." In place of ornament, which he considered to be in a state of crisis, Loos posited the effect of the material: "Never before has Cipollino marble been used in such quantities. After the fall of Rome, the quarries were forgotten and the Middle Ages and the Renaissance could work only with material taken from the buildings of the Romans. Six years ago the quarries of Euboea were rediscovered, and now the house on the Michaelerplatz is to become the first major work of architecture done in this most beautiful and magnificent of all marbles."

Adolf Loos's Haus am Michaelerplatz is the architectonic manifestation of all of the architect's axioms (or dogmas). In his theoretical work he preached the absolute rejection of any kind of decor, to be replaced by top-quality material worked with first-class craftsmanship. This can be seen in Loos's building, as can the strict separation between the business premises, with their marble cladding, and the private, anonymous living quarters above, done in simple plasterwork.

Czech, Hermann, and Wolfgang Mistelbauer. *Das Looshaus*. Vienna: Löcker & Wögenstein, 1976.

HAUS SCHEU

ADOLF LOOS
1912–1913

Unique in form for the period in which it was built, Haus Scheu represents the "first terraced apartment house in Central Europe." With this design Loos was able to provide each bedroom with a terrace facing east. The second and third floors form a single, continuous dwelling unit. The uppermost story was conceived as a separate rental apartment with its own entrance, accessible from the street. The idea for the terracing was certainly influenced by the indigenous Mediterranean architecture that Loos knew well from his travels (often undertaken in search of suitable marble). Here, too, as with his earlier house on the Michaelerplatz, Adolf Loos's design brought him great difficulties with the building authorities, this time because of the overall appearance of the façade and its lack of ornament. It was demanded that the façade be "hidden," that is to say, clothed. The owner, attorney Gustav Scheu, was forced to agree to allow plants to overgrow the façade. Much irritation was also expressed on account of the building's asymmetry.

If the outward appearance of the Scheu house may be ascribed to the influence of Mediterranean culture, the interior design is owed to the Anglo-Saxon. Time and again, in both theory and architectural practice, Loos referred back to the example of American and British habits of living. "Enlightenment came to him in America…a very young country which uses an iron technology resolutely and without excuses." The outward occasion for his visit to America was the Chicago World's Fair of 1893. During his sojourn in America, Loos also stopped in Philadelphia and then in New York. He financed his stay doing odd jobs; in New York, according to his own testimony, he also worked as an architect and furniture designer.

Disregarding his lifelong conviction that the American and British ways of life were to be preferred to the continental, one can detect the transcontinental influence especially in his concepts of interior design. In the Scheu house this is especially apparent in the fireplace nook. In general, Loos's thoughts on his so-called Raumplan (spatial plan)—i.e., the conception of architecture in its three-dimensionality and spatiality, the interlocking of spatial volumes, of higher and lower rooms, each according to purpose and significance—were inconceivable without their American and British precedents, as was also the case with the built-in furniture he propagated. Loos also paid special attention to the sanitary, hygienic aspect of American-British living. He denounced the backwardness of Central and Eastern Europe, especially that of Austria. Only the imitation of America and England would, in his opinion, lead "to the introduction of Western culture into Austria."

Rukschcio, Burkhardt, and Roland Schachel. *Leben und Werk*. Salzburg-Vienna 1982. Kurrent, Friedrich. "33 Wohnhäuser." In *Adolf Loos: Catalogue of the Exhibition*. Vienna 1989/90, 107ff.

CREMATORIUM

CLEMENS HOLZMEISTER
1921–1922

"This design was the greatest success of my life in Vienna. Because of it I was offered a chair as professor at the Academy." Thus the architect recollects his first monumental building to be executed. Although it was prohibited by the Roman Catholic Church, cremation was pushed forward by the Social Democratic Party of Vienna, which passed a resolution in 1919 to build a crematory in Vienna; for a site they chose the grounds of the sixteenth-century mannerist pleasure palace of Neugebäude. Clemens Holzmeister only received third prize in the competition held in 1920; but the municipal administration gave him the job because—as Holzmeister himself said—his design "was best suited to the area."

Holzmeister responded to the mannerist architecture of the existing building with his own expressionist architecture—which certainly shows numerous allusions to the Gothic: "I had a look at the construction site. And there was this old [palace of] Neugebäude, which made an enormous impression on me. Without windows, a wonderful architecture. A strictly unified whole. This place and those grounds, with the old trees, and the containing wall. The crenelations and merlons on top."

Holzmeister, like many other architects of the 1920s, used the expressionism of his architecture to perfect the architecture of the Gothic—just as, analogously, classicism finds its perfection in quasi modernism. With this "Gothic" expressivity, Holzmeister achieved a high degree of sacral nature and monumentality in an architectural task that, at the time, still had almost no models and had not yet evolved a typological form of its own.

Steiner, Dietmar. ". . . was man denkt, das zeichnet man. . . ." *Ein Gespräch mit Clemens Holzmeister*. In *Um Bau* 4 (1981): 61ff.

AMALIENBAD
(THE AMALIEN BATHS)

OTTO NADEL &
KARL SCHMALHOFER
1923–1926

"Imbued with the conviction that a purposeful increase in bathing facilities will encourage the populace to bathe and swim, and also contribute to the enhancement of public health, the municipal council of Vienna has, since the end of the war, not only promoted the expansion of the existing bathing facilities, but also built a series of large (new) public baths." In the "red Vienna" of the years between the wars, public health policy went hand-in-hand with Social Democratic housing and cultural policies. Equipped with the capacity to serve thirteen hundred persons at a time, as well as the "most varied bathing facilities," the Amalienbad was celebrated as one of the "largest and most modern baths in Europe."

In terms of its architecture, the "public bath," a building intended for practical use, was exalted by the municipality of Vienna in much the same way as its apartment buildings were. The interior could be described as the modern Social Democratic version of a Roman thermal bath. The exterior, an almost utopian-megalomaniacal layering of architectural masses, became a monument to hygiene and cleanliness. Crowned with a water tower reminiscent of a castle keep, which at the same time is a clock tower showing the time, the function of the architecture was above all to signify the "new era." To the exterior of this monument to municipal concern for hygiene and cleanliness, the inside responds with the aestheticization of the cleansing process. Bathing and washing are liberated from the sphere of the purely utilitarian, necessary, and healthy, and transported into the sphere of the aesthetic. "Outwardly, the building presents itself as a monumental, cubic mass. To the original outer appearance of the building corresponds the inner architectonic design, which offers proof that functionality means beauty. A cheerful, harmonic effect is achieved by means of colorful wall cladding and mosaic work."

In its clear status-competition with the haut-bourgeois spa and bathing facilities of the latter half of the nineteenth century, the overall effect is one of a building removed from reality, a downright exotic architectonic counterworld. The result, as with those older buildings, is an architecture that is an experience in itself and an uncommon aesthetic attraction.

Das Bäderwesen der Gemeinde Wien. Vienna: Wiener Magistrat, n.d., but before 1930.
Achleitner, Friedrich. *Österreichische Architektur im 20. Jahrhundert. Ein Führer in vier Bänden,* vol. III/1, Salzburg-Vienna: Residenz, 1990, 284ff.

KARL MARX HOF

KARL EHN 1927–1930

The Karl Marx Hof was one of the largest housing projects to be built as part of the social housing program of the Social Democratic municipal administration of Vienna during the period between the wars. Designed to encompass 1,382 apartments, it was the "most gigantic architectural task ever undertaken within the context of an apartment complex." Apart from the all-dominating middle section, built in the form of a main courtyard complex and given special emphasis by six tower superstructures, the two "wings" of the Karl Marx Hof followed the customary pattern of 1920s social apartment buildings in the municipality of Vienna. These always featured a periphery of buildings enclosing a large inner courtyard. The stairways leading to the apartments were entered not from the street, but from these inner courtyards. This concept was a conscious departure from the nineteenth-century tradition of workers' apartment buildings. During the 1920s, an attempt was made to design the inner courtyards to be more and more like a park, that is, to pare down to a minimum the percentage of the surface used for buildings. In the Karl Marx Hof, a mere 18 percent of the overall surface was used for buildings: everything else was lawn or garden space, which also contained the ancillary living facilities, such as laundries, baths, and kindergartens.

The architecture itself always strove for eloquent expressivity, as an architectonic demonstration of the role of the Social Democratic party. The main courtyard, previously reserved as a form expressing the dignity of the castle, was appropriated as an expression of the dignity of the social housing project; the statue of the ruler made way for the monument to the worker or peasant (here, the center is occupied by the "Sower"). The allegorical glorification of the ruling class now yielded to the personification of the achievements of Social Democracy. Standing upon the four capstones above the oversized main arches that lead through the middle section are the figures of Freedom, Welfare, Enlightenment, and Physical Culture.

Many of the architects of the Viennese social housing projects, including Karl Ehn, were students of Otto Wagner; following his teachings, they included in many of the so-called superblocks such significantly Wagnerian features as symmetry and axiality, as well as the monumentalization for which he also strove in his apartment-building architecture.

Der Karl Marx Hof. Die Wohnhausanlage der Gemeinde Wien auf der Hagenwiese in Heiligenstadt.
Vienna: Wiener Stadtbauamt, 1930.

HAUS WENZGASSE

JOSEF FRANK 1930

Josef Frank was a champion of the single-family house. Unlike Adolf Loos, however, Josef Frank did not concern himself with the development of a spatial plan in the sense of the interlocking of architectural shapes, but only in the sense of pathfinding, that is, the realization of his idea of the house "as path and place." Frank's sequences of rooms are not linked to one another by means of axes; rather, he created a spatial system determined by paths and places. "I should like to explain the organization of the modern house as a path; by that I mean: the essential thing about a good house is the manner in which one enters the house and walks through the house….In this regard one of the most important rules is that this path be continuous, that the straight line be broken at characteristic points, and that each turn appear motivated; above all it is necessary that we never go back and that no path has to be taken twice."

The rear of Haus Wenzgasse reveals yet another characteristic of Frank's architecture, the link between architecture and nature. "The nature surrounding the house should make the transition, in a discreet fashion, into the house itself."

If we compare Haus Wenzgasse with other single-family homes by Josef Frank, it will be clear that the formal-aesthetic modernity achieved here (in the sense of the classical modernism of the 1920s) is almost accidental, illusory. This is particularly the case in the main façade; and here, too, upon closer analysis, the way in which modernism is contradicted comes to light. In opposition to thoroughgoing composition, to the gridlike, to the rationally planned and uniform, we find in Frank a certain aleatory quality, an almost mannerist admixture of forms (the various window shapes alone are worthy of particular attention). Frank's reply to functionalism, to the "synchronization of industry and art," was his concept of the manifoldly accidental, so to speak; and he countered uniformity with a contradictory complexity.

Frank, Josef. *Das Haus als Weg und Platz*. Reprinted in *Josef Frank. 1885–1967. Catalogue of the Exhibition*. Vienna: Hochschule für angewandte Kunst, 1981, 36ff.

HAUS WITTGENSTEIN

LUDWIG WITTGENSTEIN & PAUL ENGELMANN 1926–1928

In 1926, Margarethe Stonborough-Wittgenstein, a sister of the philosopher Ludwig Wittgenstein, commissioned the architect Paul Engelmann, a former student of Adolf Loos, to build a new, freestanding house in Vienna's third municipal district. In that same year, Ludwig Wittgenstein was called in as consulting architect, even though he had no professional training in the field. It is possible that his sister did this to help him overcome the crisis in which he had found himself since World War I. By dint of his extremely forceful personality, Ludwig Wittgenstein dominated the planning from the moment he was engaged, especially with regard to details.

Inspection of the executed building shows rather clearly that the basic structure, with its interlocking of cubic architectural shapes, may be ascribed to Engelmann. All too plain are the analogies to the architecture of his teacher, Adolf Loos. As far as the spatial program and dimensions are concerned, Margarethe Stonborough-Wittgenstein seems to have set the tone, since it all corresponds to quite traditional, haut-bourgeois notions of living. A large central hall with accompanying dining and living rooms, an imposing entrance hall—all of this exactly fit her lifestyle. Ludwig Wittgenstein's philosophical-aesthetic concepts of design come into play in the precise exactitude of the general proportions and in the exact precision of the particular details.

The architectonic solution that resulted is on the whole quite unique. In terms of functionality and dimensional principles, the rooms are worthy of Josef Hoffmann; they are enclosed in an outer shell that unmistakably bears the "imprint" of Adolf Loos, Hoffmann's bitter opponent—and all of this is expressed in an architectural language that has been proportioned and detailed with philosophical exactitude.

Leitner, Bernhard. *The Architecture of Ludwig Wittgenstein. A Documentation.* Halifax-London: The Press of the Nova Scotia College of Art and Design, 1973.

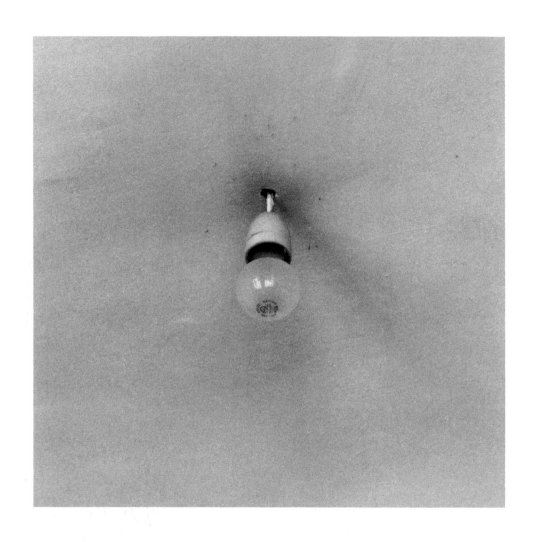

NOTES

1. Adolf Loos, "Die Potemkin'sche Stadt." In *Die Potemkin'sche Stadt. Verschollene Schriften 1897–1933,* ed. Adolf Opel (Vienna: Prachner, 1983), 55ff.

2. Ludwig Hevesi, "Das Haus der Sezession," in *Acht Jahre Sezession. Kritik-Polemik-Chronik* (Vienna: Konegen, 1906), 63ff.

3. *Wiener Zeitung,* December 25, 1857.

4. Alice Strobl, *Das k. k. Waffenmuseum im Arsenal. Der Bau und seine künstlerische Ausschmückung* (Vienna: Böhlau, 1961), 107.

5. C. von Vincenti, "Der Reichsrathspalast," in *Wiener Kunst-Renaissance. Studien und Charakteristiken* (Vienna: Gerold, 1876), 69ff.

6. Karl Weiß, *Festschrift aus Anlaß der Vollendung des neuen Rathhauses* (Vienna: Selbstverlag d. Gemeinderates, 1883), 50ff.

7. Ibid.

8. Ibid.

9. Ibid.

10. J. v. Falke, quoted in *Festschrift bei Gelegenheit der feierlichen Enthüllung seines Denkmals im k. k. Österreichischen Museum für Kunst und Industrie,* H. Freiherr von Ferstel (Vienna: Verlag d. k.k. Österreichischen Museums, 1884), 20.

11. J. Burckhardt, *Die Kultur der Renaissance in Italien. Ein Versuch,* vol. 1, 9th ed. (Leipzig: Scholtze, 1904), 234.

12. Wenzel Herzig, *Die angewandte oder praktische Aesthetik oder die Theorie der dekorativen Architektur* (Leipzig: 1873), 9ff.

13. Burckhardt, *Die Kultur der Renaissance in Italien,* vol. 2, 77.

14. Ibid.

15. Thus the titles to several of Burckhardt's chapters.

16. Otto Wagner, *Moderne Architektur* (Vienna: Schroll, 1896), 38.

17. Otto Wagner, *Einige Skizzen, Projekte und ausgeführte Bauwerke* (Vienna: Schroll, 1890), Foreword.

18. Ibid.

19. Ibid.

20. Ibid.

21. Otto Wagner, *Die Baukunst unserer Zeit;* this is the title under which the fourth edition of *Moderne Architektur* was published. (Vienna: Schroll, 1914), 87.

22. Wagner, *Moderne Architektur,* 62f.

23. "Das neue Haus. Zur Bauvollendung des neuen Postsparkassengebäudes," in *Neues Wiener Journal* (13 December 1906): 3; and Ludwig Hevesi, "Der Neubau der Postsparkasse," in *Altkunst-Neukunst. Wien 1894–1908* (Vienna: Konegen, 1909), 245ff.

24. "Das neue Haus. Zur Bauvollendung des neuen Postsparkassengebäudes," in *Neues Wiener Journal* (13 December 1906): 3.

25. "Architektonische Details der Wiener Stadtbahn," in *Der Architekt* IV (1898): 27.

26. Ibid.

27. Otto Wagner, *Moderne Architektur,* 58.

28. Hermann Muthesius, *Wirtschaftsformen im Kunstgewerbe* (Berlin: no publisher, 1908), 10ff.

29. Richard Schaukal, *Vom Geschmack. Zeitgemäße Laienpredigten über das Thema Kultur* (Munich: 1910), 68.

30. Adolf Loos, "Ornament und Erziehung," in *Sämtliche Schriften, Bd. I* (Vienna-Munich: Herold, 1962), 392ff.

31. Adolf Loos, "Hands off!" in *Trotzdem* (1934; Reprint, Vienna: Prachner, 1982), 134.

32. Adolf Loos, "Ornament und Verbrechen," in *Trotzdem,* 82.

33. Hartwig Fischel, "Möbelentwürfe der Empire und Biedermeierzeit," in *Kunst und Kunsthandwerk* XXIII (1920): 100.

34. Adolf Loos, "Ornament und Erziehung," 393.

35. Adolf Loos, "Architektur," in *Trotzdem,* 99.

36. Wilhelm Schölermann, "Café Museum," in *Kontroversen. Adolf Loos im Spiegel der Zeitgenossen,* ed. Adolf Opel (Vienna: Prachner, 1985), 9.

37. Adolf Loos, "Architektur," 92.

38. Adolf Loos, "Ornament und Verbrechen," 78f.

39. Ibid., 79.

40. Sigmund Freud, "Die 'kulturelle' Sexualmoral und die moderne Nervösität" (1908), in *Sigmund Freud Studienausgabe,* vol. IX (Frankfurt: Fischer, 1974), 18.

41. Adolf Loos, "Ornament und Verbrechen," 79.

42. Adolf Loos, "Ornament und Erziehung," 174.

43. Ibid., 177.

44. Adolf Loos, "Ornament und Verbrechen," 88.

45. Ibid., 87.

46. Commentary in *Kritik und Revue,* 24 July 1911. Quotation from Hermann Czech and Wolfgang Mistelbauer, *Das Looshaus* (Vienna: Löcker & Wögenstein, 1976), 86.

47. Ibid., 79.

48. Adolf Loos, "Architektur," 100.

49. Hermann Czech and Wolfgang Mistelbauer, *Das Looshaus,* 75.

50. Adolf Loos, "Von einem armen, reichen Manne," in *Ins Leere gesprochen* (1921; Reprint, Vienna: Prachner, 1981), 198ff.

51. Adolf Loos, "Die Interieurs in der Rotunde," in *Ins Leere gesprochen,* 77.

52. Anton Weber, "Wiener Wohnungs und Sozialpolitik," in *Das Neue Wien,* vol. I (Vienna: 1926), 193.

53. "Die Gemeinde Wien und die bildende Kunst," in *Das Neue Wien,* vol. II (Vienna: Elbemühl, 1927), 150.

54. Josef Bittner, *Die Wohnhausbauten,* vol. 1 of *Neubauten der Stadt Wien* (Vienna-Leipzig-New York: Gerlach & Wiedling, 1926), 3.

55. Josef Frank, "Der Volkswohnungspalast. Eine Rede, anläßlich der Grundsteinlegung, die nicht gehalten wurde," in *Der Aufbau* 1 (1926): 108.

56. Josef Frank, "Das Haus als Weg und Platz," in *Josef Frank 1885–1967. Catalogue of the Exhibition* (Vienna: Hochschule für angewandte Kunst, 1981), 36ff.

57. Josef Frank, "Akzidentismus" (1958). Reprinted in *Josef Frank 1885–1967,* 236ff.

58. Family reminiscences of Hermine Wittgenstein. Excerpts printed in *The Architecture of Ludwig Wittgenstein,* by Bernhard Leitner (Halifax-London: The Press of the Nova Scotia College of Art and Design, 1973), 17ff.